Joss Bennathan

Joss Bennathan is a theatre director and artistic director of Present Moment theatre company. He also directs regularly at various British drama schools, as well as producing festivals of devised young people's theatre in the UK and USA.

A former head of Drama at an East London comprehensive school and Ofsted inspector, Joss was an area leader for both GCSE and A-level Drama and Theatre Studies for a number of years. He was secondary Drama consultant for both the London Boroughs of Barking and Dagenham and Newham, and continues to advise and mentor Drama teachers. He has written education resource materials for Arc Theatre and the Lyric Hammersmith, amongst others. His books, *Developing Drama Skills 11–14* and *Performance Power*, are widely used in UK schools and colleges and abroad.

MAKING THEATRE

The Frazzled Drama Teacher's Guide to Devising

Joss Bennathan

NICK HERN BOOKS
London
www.nickhernbooks.co.uk

Making Theatre: The Frazzled Drama Teacher's Guide to Devising
first published in Great Britain in 2013
by Nick Hern Books Limited,
The Glasshouse, 49a Goldhawk Road, London W12 8QP

Cover photo by Mark Tunnicliffe (marktunnicliffe.com)

Designed and typeset by Nick Hern Books, London
Printed and bound in Great Britain by CPI Group (UK) Ltd

A CIP catalogue record for this book
is available from the British Library

ISBN 978 1 84842 305 3

For Gracie

Contents

Acknowledgements and Thanks   xi

Introduction   1

Part 1: Preparation

1. How do I determine the best way of grouping students?   11
2. How do I manage and monitor several groups rehearsing
    simultaneously?   20
3. The group I am teaching has very low-level skills and
    very little ability to work productively for any length of
    time. How do I raise them to the required standard?   23
4. How long should the rehearsal process be?   26
5. How do I enable students to avoid shallow, clichéd work?   29
6. How do I ensure that boys engage and attain?   31
7. How do I include the erratic attender without jeopardising
    the work of the others?   35
8. What degree of directing and guidance is appropriate?   37
9. To what extent is it appropriate to use existing scripts, and
    do these benefit or limit candidates' attainment?   39
10. The exam specification we use stipulates a theme.
    Doesn't this limit what I can do?   41
11. Should some subjects, themes and styles be avoided?   42

12. To what extent do costumes, set and lighting impress
     an examiner?   45

13. My best student last year did not get the marks they
     deserved. What happened? How do I avoid it this year?   48

14. I worry that an inappropriate audience response will distract
     the visiting examiner or undermine the performers. What
     can I do to avoid this situation?   50

Part 2: Making

Overview   55

Structures for Making Theatre

1. **Transgressive Love**   62

2. **Reportage**   70

3. **Montage**   77

4. **We All Come From Somewhere Else**   84

5. **No Inspiration Required**   94

6. **This Woman's Work**   102

7. **The Multiple Protagonist**   109

8. **The Third Way**   115

9. **Same Starting Point, Different Outcomes**   125

10. **No Feeling, No Emotion**   133

An Overview of Stage 3: Rehearsing   143

Student Resource Sheets

1. Creating a Character: Getting Started   147

2. Making Theatre: Getting Started   148

3. Developing a Character in Depth and Detail   149

4. Making Theatre: Depth and Detail   150

Part 3: Refining, Troubleshooting and Finishing

Overview 153

1.   Audibility 157

Can you hear them? 157

Can you understand what they are saying? 159

2.   Characterisation 163

Is the student convincing in the role? 163

Does the student move in a way that is appropriate to the
character, in general or at a particular moment? 164

Does the student use a vocabulary appropriate to the
character? 165

Does the student know why they are speaking? 167

Does the characterisation lack depth and detail? 169

Has the student considered the character's backstory? 169

Is the student commenting on the character? 170

Are the different characters being played actually different
from each other? 173

Is the student gesturing too much? Or gesturing
inappropriately? 174

Is the student's face expressive enough? 175

That student is just wandering around the stage! What do I
do to stop this? 177

3.   Visibility 178

Is there an awareness of the importance of how the piece
is staged? 178

4.   Communication 181

Is the ensemble energised? 182

Is the ensemble focused on and attuned to each other? 184

Why is that direct address not working? 185

Why is this scene not working? 188

Are the students telling rather than showing? 188

What is going on in the scene and why?   191

What is the point of this scene?   192

Does the scene lack tension?   193

Is a student overacting? Are they underacting?   196

How are the group managing transitions and
performance conventions?   198

Everything is happening so fast it's incomprehensible!
What can I do?   200

Does the work lack presence and a sense of occasion?   202

Is the narrative clear?   203

Preparation and Stimulus Material   205

Group-work Preference
Scheme of Work Audit
Ensuring Boys' Attainment
Transgressive Love: 'Vrbana Bridge'
Montage: Extract from 'The Trial'
We All Come From Somewhere Else: Interview Questions
We All Come From Somewhere Else:
    Arrival: Personal Testimony
No Inspiration Required: Pair Exercise (A) and Trio Exercise
No Inspiration Required: Solo Exercise (A) and
    Pair Exercises (B) and (C)
No Inspiration Required: Solo Exercise (B)
This Woman's Work: Cold Dark Matter: An Exploded View
The Third Way: 'Pirate Jenny'
Same Starting Point, Different Outcomes:
    Notice of Change of Name
No Feeling, No Emotion: Military Drill
No Feeling, No Emotion: Varnado Simpson's Account
No Feeling, No Emotion: My Lai: Personal Testimony
'Rehearsing is not about getting it right . . .'

Index of Exercises   223

Acknowledgements

The author and publisher would like to thank the following for permission to use copyright material:

Jill Sobule (www.jillsobule.com) for the lyrics to 'Vrbana Bridge', written and composed by Jill Sobule (Feel My Pain Music/ASCAP) and Robin Eaton (Left Right Left Music/BMI/Admin BMG); David Wyllie for the extract from his translation of *The Trial* by Franz Kafka (the full translation can be found at www.kafka-online.info/the-trial.html); London Transport Museum for oral testimony from their booklet, *Sun a-Shine, Rain a-Fall: London Transport's West Indian Workforce*; Pearson Education Ltd for extracts from *Motherland* by Elyse Dodgson, and Pearson Education Inc., Upper Saddle River, NJ, for extracts from *Four Hours in My Lai* (1st edition © 2003) by Michael Bilton; Cornelia Parker and the Frith Street Gallery for *Cold Dark Matter: An Exploded View*; MDS (Hire & Copyright) Ltd on behalf of Universal Edition for Marc Blitzstein's translation of Bertolt Brecht's lyrics to the Kurt Weill song, 'Pirate Jenny'; EdExcel for the quote from the Chief Examiner's report on GCSE Drama, 2012; and Ofsted for the quote from the report, *Boys' Achievement in Secondary Schools* (© Crown copyright, 2003).

Every effort has been made to trace the copyright holders, but if any have been inadvertently overlooked, the publisher will be pleased to make the necessary arrangements at the first opportunity.

Thanks to:

- Jules Tipton, who has been an invaluable sounding board and source of expertise throughout the preparation of this book. Jules has worked with me on several devised theatre projects, as well as being the associate director of Present Moment, for whom I am artistic director.

- Cath Cook and Shannen Owen, two fine drama teachers, whose insight and support have helped shape my practice and provided some of the ideas and approaches in this book.

- Carole Pluckrose and Clifford Oliver, of Arc Theatre, whose advice and guidance are always invaluable and much appreciated.

- Kate Chadwick, Rachel Coleman, Shannen Owen (again) and Maria Waldron for their wisdom and practical advice. All four appeared in a DVD I made for the London Borough of Newham on how to manage the devising process.

- Andrew Mutter, formerly Arts Advisor for the London Borough of Newham, commissioned that DVD, as well as somehow finding the funding for the four celebrations of devised theatre that I directed and coordinated for Newham Arts Festival.

- All the Drama teachers in the London Borough of Newham that made devised theatre pieces for *The Genre Project*, *The Reportage Project*, *The Adaptation Project* and *We All Come From Somewhere Else*.

- Jane Robinson, formerly Gifted and Talented Advisor for the London Borough of Newham, who worked alongside me on the annual projects for 'gifted and talented' Year 9 students. Also to the following people, who directed for those various projects: Orlessa Altass, Chris Buckingham, Deni Francis, Alison Goldie, Sheryl Malcolm, Abdul Shayek, Kieron Singh, John Lang, Simon Rivers and Oscar Ward.

- Ian Starling, then Senior English Advisor in the London Borough of Barking and Dagenham, for my ongoing work in that borough, as well as all the teachers in that borough who invited me into their classrooms and drama studios.

- Robin Kaplan, for commissioning me to make devised theatre pieces in Key West, Florida – and for creating the music for those pieces.

- Danièle Sanderson, Paul Clarkson, Lise Olsen and Alex Taylor at Birmingham School of Acting, and Sally Ann Gritton and Jacqui Somerville at Mountview Academy for Theatre Arts. Many of the activities and exercises in this book have come from the 'off text' exercises I used when directing scenes and plays with students on their professional theatre training courses.

- My daughter, Ella Turner, for her forensic analysis, and also to Sue Quirk, Annie Tunnicliffe and Joan Walker for their proofreading skills.

- Ginny Spooner for her guidance regarding examination-board specifications.

- Nick Hern, Matt Applewhite and everyone at Nick Hern Books, who have supported this book from commission to publication.

- And finally all the actors: professional, in training, in schools and in youth theatre, with whom I have honed my ideas, learned from my experiences and developed my practice.

Introduction

You wake with a start, in a sweat. Your pulse is racing. You are clenching your teeth so tightly that your jaw and your temples ache. Confused images dance before your bleary eyes: being attacked, being chased, being out of control in a situation where you're meant to be competent.

Relax. Or try to. Everyone has work-related nightmares, presumably because somewhere in there, even the most outwardly confident person fears being judged, found wanting, exposed. Such nightmares are usually job-specific. For example, the actor's nightmare takes various forms: finding yourself in the wrong play, in the wrong costume or in none at all (inappropriate and embarrassing nudity is a classic feature of such dreams), not knowing lines which were once so familiar.

As exam season looms or progresses, what are the Drama teacher's nightmares? Do yours focus on process or product? What is the worst that you can imagine when your students present their devised piece to an audience and an examiner? And, leading up to that, what is your nightmare vision of the rehearsal process?

I run courses for Drama teachers on a regular basis. Often, I ask them to create a scene that dramatises their collective nightmares. It's fun, it breaks the ice, but it also has a serious purpose. The naming of fears makes them more manageable. It is always a relief to discover that other people feel and experience the same anxieties and frustrations as you do. Take a few minutes now, and list the features of yours. Here are some that I polled from a random selection of Drama teachers, plus a

1

few of my own. You can work out for yourself which apply to process, which to performance and which to both:

- Chronically absent, perpetually late students who seem to have no sense of urgency, of time or of the looming performance date.
- The level of noise as you attempt to work with several groups in a space way too small for purpose.
- Being crushed by the weight of exam-board paperwork.
- Trying, Alice-in-Wonderland style, to work out the logic of the subjective or downright unfair marks awarded last year and deliver what is required.
- Students mumbling and shuffling on stage, with no sense of how to arrange themselves to ensure audience visibility.
- Ghastly sub-soap-opera melodramas with far too much shouting and arm-waving.
- Dysfunctional groups who can't or won't work together.
- Unexpected improvisations.
- Parents or carers taking their child on that once-in-a-lifetime holiday during the exam preparation period.
- Scenes that have made their point but go on and on and on.

I work on the assumption that you tend to feel over-responsible and are hugely conscientious because, in my experience, the vast majority of teachers do and are, despite what is inferred by a succession of educational initiatives. I also work on the assumption that your school puts enormous pressure on its teachers to set targets, and to improve or maintain results while probably paying too little attention to the specific demands and needs of externally examined Drama preparation. Enhancement and revision classes in other subjects eat up time after school and at lunchtime, when those precious additional rehearsals used to take place. Is it any wonder that, come examination season, the Drama teacher is rarely seen in the staffroom, and when they are, looks haggard, shaky and inclined to snarl at imaginary enemies? Home life is no better. Partners are neglected. Children and pets go unfed. I exaggerate, but only just. Managing the devising process is often demanding, difficult and challenging. It can lead even highly competent teachers to feel disempowered. However, help is at hand. This book is designed to provide a framework and process that will, most of the time, avoid common pitfalls and prevent the nightmare becoming reality.

It's a framework that is based on my experience and observation over the last quarter century. I was a Drama teacher. Now I'm a theatre director. Along the way, I've been an area leader for both GCSE Drama and A-level Drama and Theatre Studies, examining devised drama throughout London and the South East and mentoring and monitoring other examiners. I've run courses for Drama teachers. I've advised and inspected Drama. I've curated and mentored festivals of devised secondary Drama. On a couple of occasions, I've been called in to rescue GCSE groups who, for various reasons, required a crash course in basic skills plus needed to learn how to devise, whilst in the throes of doing so! On my travels, I've noticed how the same issues are encountered by a range of teachers, irrespective of their experience or the environment within which they work.

This book is intended for all those who help young people make devised theatre, particularly for those who teach an exam specification that culminates in an externally examined performance. GCSE Drama and BTEC (First) classes tend to be larger (and younger) than post-sixteen groups, hence they present specific managerial challenges. But the principles and approaches can be used to benefit students on A-level courses, diploma and foundation courses, and in higher education as well as in youth theatre groups.

The first part of this book, Preparation, is framed as a series of questions from a range of Drama teachers, whether the novice coping with her first exam season, the non-specialist or the exhausted veteran. Find answers to these questions and we begin to build the necessary, solid foundations that underpin devised theatre.

- How do I determine the best way of grouping students?
- How do I manage and monitor several groups rehearsing simultaneously?
- The group I am teaching has very low-level skills and very little ability to work productively for any length of time. How do I raise them to the required standard?

- How long should the rehearsal process be?
- How do I enable students to avoid shallow, clichéd work?
- How do I ensure that boys engage and attain?
- How do I include the erratic attender without jeopardising the work of the others?
- What degree of directing and guidance is appropriate?
- To what extent is it appropriate to use existing scripts, and do these benefit or limit candidates' attainment?
- The exam specification we use stipulates a theme. Doesn't this limit what I can do?
- Should some subjects, themes and styles be avoided?
- To what extent do costumes, set and lighting impress an examiner?
- My best student last year did not get the marks they deserved. What happened? How do I avoid it this year?
- I worry that an inappropriate audience response will distract the visiting examiner or undermine the performers. What can I do to avoid this situation?

The second part of the book, Making, provides ten structures for devised work, to meet the needs of different students and situations. These include a range of starting points and stimuli as well as suggesting a model for the devising rehearsal process that enables you to monitor quality and progress throughout that process.

The third part, Refining, Troubleshooting and Finishing, provides a range of stand-alone exercises. These can – and I believe should – be part of your overall curriculum, in order that students may demonstrate their understanding of the following in their work, whether short, rapidly assembled scenes in class or extended devised pieces:

- Voice and movement.
- Characterisation, whether physicalisation, status or appropriate vocabulary.
- The intended effect on audience.

- Communication: within the ensemble and between performers and audience (I use the word 'ensemble' in preference to 'cast' because, regardless of the type of piece being created, ensemble suggests a commitment to working together which cast does not).
- The relationship between style, content and form.
- Transitions between scenes and performance conventions.
- Narrative economy and clarity.

These exercises can also be assigned, used or revisited at any stage in the devising process.

The overarching aim is to maximise attainment by creating the best possible pieces of theatre and to enable you to manage the process in the most effective, least stressful way possible.

My framework for devised theatre is based on a series of guiding principles. These will be discussed and demonstrated throughout this book but they are worth summarising here:

- The first principle is that making theatre is not the same as teaching Drama. After all, no one says 'I am going to the drama tonight.' Making theatre involves creating something primarily for an audience rather than for the participant. This subtle but important distinction leads to a shift in emphasis in the effective Drama teacher's practice. It is easy to get lost in target-setting, assessment objectives and so on. We forget our own experience as spectators, readers and audience, which is that what engages and sustains our interest is the simple desire to find out 'What happens next?'
- The second principle is that it is important to understand the difference between devising theatre and improvisation, whether spontaneous or prepared. Again, it is easy to get lost in ensuring that students understand and use the explorative strategies that improvisation units require. We forget that these must be viewed as means of approaching the elements of Drama and medium of Drama, rather than an end in themselves. For it is

the understanding of the elements and medium of Drama which leads to outstanding devised work.

- The third is that we cannot reasonably expect young people to know how to rehearse for extended periods, nor how to structure and create effective theatre, unless they have been taught how to do so. If students are used to making a quick piece of theatre in a single lesson, then showing it, evaluating it and moving on, they are unlikely to be able to manage an extended rehearsal process and the editing, refining, reworking and experimentation that is required.

- The fourth, it follows, is that, throughout the devising process, the Drama teacher has an obligation to monitor, shape, advise and, where necessary say: 'No.' Would your colleagues in the English department suggest to someone that their extended essay be handed in in eight weeks' time without providing structure and guidance and without expecting drafts and redrafts during that period? Of course not.

- The fifth and final overarching principle is that a framework within which to function gives students creative freedom rather than limits it. It provides a springboard. Once, having watched incoherent, mumbled, uncertain devised work in progress, the class's Drama teacher airily assured me that he didn't structure or guide because he didn't want to impede his students' expression of their creativity. I found myself enquiring, through gritted teeth, how they were supposed to express their creativity if they were not given the tools to do so? Surely that's like saying, 'Here's a slab of marble. Sculpt it with your teeth and fingernails'?

I am not suggesting that any or all of these principles outlined above are new to you. I am not asking you to reinvent the wheel or suggesting that everything you know or do is wrong. However, I hope that this book will provide the experienced teacher with an opportunity to step back and reflect and, perhaps, recharge. Also that it will provide the less-experienced teacher, particularly those working in isolation, with a path through the forest.

To teach is to work in a state of constant flux. At the time of writing, the powers that be seem to be losing interest in vocational qualifications. Amendments to the national curriculum threaten how and indeed if arts subjects, including Drama, are taught in schools. AS- and A-level specifications are likely to change in response to the demands of universities. Yet wherever and however Drama occurs, some element of devised performance is bound to remain. Regardless of what course is being delivered, we owe it to ourselves to make the process as manageable and as stress-free as possible. We owe it to our students to give them the tools and the skills to reach above and beyond their own expectations and aspirations. If we do not do these things we fail our students and ourselves.

Part One

PREPARATION

1. How do I determine the best way of grouping students?

The first thing to acknowledge is that this is actually several questions wrapped up in one.

- Does it mean what are the arguments for friendship groups versus teacher-assigned groups?
- Does it mean whether high-ability students should be combined with other high achievers?
- Does it mean how to accommodate the individual who has never shown much interest, enthusiasm or talent?
- Or does it mean what to do with the individual who is an erratic attender?

There is a maxim in theatre that once you've got the casting right, you're ninety per cent of the way there. In school and college Drama, the same principle applies regarding who works with whom. This is why the conscientious teacher spends so much time pondering the answers to the questions above. My contention is this: get the group dynamic right and the rest falls into place.

Of course, the extent to which the selection of groups is your choice depends on your standing with the class. In theory, it is a fundamental principle that Drama involves working with everyone in the class, not just their friends. In practice, if you've taken over the group recently and if, to make the task harder, they have had several short-term Drama teachers, then theory flies out the window. You need to make a pragmatic decision. If it's a choice between getting some work out of them or no work at all, then let them choose the groups they work in. There is a time and place to pick your battles. This isn't one of them. You have enough to do without quelling mutiny every lesson. Do not waste precious energy raging about how things should be. Deal with how things are. However, this is not to say you cannot influence a student self-selecting process. Of which, more later.

Irrespective of how groups are selected and who makes that selection, the answer to the question, 'What is the most effective size of groups?' is simple: the smaller the better. Five or fewer. There are several sensible, practical reasons for this. Firstly, exam boards stipulate that the length of the final piece should relate to the number of performers. A group of three have a far better chance of creating an impressive fifteen-minute piece than a group of six have of sustaining a piece for half an hour. Secondly, the smaller the group, the more opportunity there is for each candidate to have sufficient stage time to show what they can do. Thirdly, small groups galvanise creativity because they require a more imaginative approach. Therefore, the students in the group are obliged to pay far more attention to such vital components as the relationship between style, content and form. Finally – and this is crucial – group work is *hard*! The greater the number involved, the harder it gets. Think back to the last time *you* were asked to perform a group task, perhaps at an INSET day or on a course. How well did *your* group manage the negotiation involved? How did you decide who should be the scribe or who would report back to the whole group? Who kept the group on task or merrily subverted the process? Did you feel your ideas were encouraged and heard? Were decisions made consensually or by majority decision, and was that actually discussed or did it just evolve? I could go on but you take my point. Now, bear in mind that, as adults, there was probably a certain level of social skills and a degree of willingness to accomplish whatever the task was. Also bear in mind that you were probably only required to work together for half an hour or so, while we are asking our students to work together every lesson for the weeks and weeks that comprise an extended rehearsal period.

In 1965, Bruce Tuckman observed that group development occurs in four stages:

- Forming
- Storming
- Norming
- Performing

Every Drama teacher who has heard the wail, 'Miss! I can't work with her' knows that rehearsal groups often get stuck somewhere between the forming and the storming, with the emphasis on storming. If the group dynamic isn't right, you spend your time as a cross between a fire-fighter and an arbitrator. It's exhausting. So how do we do our best to ensure that our students attain the norming and performing phases?

As a director, putting together a creative team or a cast, I often ask myself how will this family – or tribe – work? Chemistry is hard to define and deconstruct but not impossible, especially when you have prior knowledge. And you do. It is simply a question of how to apply it. We spend a lot of time with new classes establishing what might be called the foundation skills – those that are necessary for meaningful Drama to take place in an ordered and supportive environment. (With some groups, heaven knows, we have to keep revisiting them.) We are told, rightly, by a range of inspectors, advisors and experts that the various abilities to concentrate, cooperate, negotiate, listen and so on are not indications of attainment. However, that does not mean that we should underestimate the impact they have on attainment.

If you've been teaching a group for any length of time, you will have instilled in your students the ability to evaluate and reflect on their work and the work of others. Constantly, I hear teachers asking, 'What worked well?' and 'What would have improved the work?' focusing – again, rightly – on students' demonstration of their understanding of Drama skills. Far less frequently do we extend this discussion to explore *why* something worked well – which is to say, what are the foundation skills which underpin successful work or sabotage less successful work? In Tuckman's terms, did they reach the performing phase? Were they able to find a shared vision and the ability to stand on their own feet with minimal intervention from you?

The aim, then, is to ensure that students are able to work productively towards a common goal. The moment you begin to consider constructing groups from this perspective, life gets easier. The first step is to audit their foundation skills.

In a previous book, I suggested that the fundamental skills for you to judge and for students to self-assess were as follows:

- Ability to concentrate.
- Ability to work outside friendship groups.
- Ability to negotiate.
- Ability to work individually.
- Ability to work in a pair.

- Ability to work as part of a whole group.
- Ability to work within a small group.
- Ability to follow a series of instructions.
- Ability to translate instructions into action.
- Ability to work with a sense of common purpose.
- Ability to work with sensitivity to the needs of others.
- Listening/retention skills.
- Ability to overcome physical inhibitions and reserve.
- Individual/collective physical control and coordination.
- Basic character movement.
- Observation skills.

Use that list as the basis for this exercise or formulate your own list. Just make sure that you focus on foundation skills rather than Drama knowledge, skills or understanding. Apply the list to the students in your group, one by one. I recommend keeping your rating system as simple as possible. Do they demonstrate the specified ability always, often, sometimes or never? That should suffice. Allow yourself the option of 'I don't know', if you genuinely don't – and you may not, especially if you are not familiar with the group. (However, if you don't know, the answer is probably *sometimes*. Generally, those students who are *never* able to follow a series of instructions or those who *always* concentrate are easy to identify!)

We all know the phrase 'Too may cooks spoil the broth'. We all know the problem with groups comprising students with a lot of ideas and limited listening or negotiation skills. Systematising this knowledge – as you have done in the exercise above – provides a sense of plausible combinations for group work. That is step one.

Step two is to ask students to assess themselves, using the same criteria. Good managers enlist their staff in decision-making, rather than despotically imposing their will, even if they have the authority to make the choice. So do good teachers. If, as mentioned earlier, your situation requires student-selected performance groups, it is even more important that they assess themselves because it helps them to focus on the task: to create as good a piece of theatre as possible. Despite occasional appearances to the contrary, most people want to succeed: problems occur when they think they cannot or don't know how to do so. (This is discussed in more detail in response to Question 3.) By making the need to find the best groups to achieve your common aim explicit, students are more likely to accept that working with mates is not always the best choice to make. Of course, you may not agree with a student's self-assessment and their peers may not either. But the very fact that an individual over- or underestimates their skills can and should be incorporated into your assignment of groups. It's also worth asking students to work in pairs, with someone that they know and trust, assessing each other.

Self-awareness is a good thing to develop above and beyond the Drama curriculum. However, to create effective functional performance groups, we must dig deeper still. Step three is to look at how individual strengths and weaknesses may complement or clash. Because a rehearsal process is a group process, systems such as Belbin Team Roles – designed specifically to identify people's behavioural strengths and weaknesses in the workplace – are highly useful. Belbin suggests that any functional group needs a balance of the following roles:

- Completer finisher
- Coordinator
- Implementer
- Monitor evaluator
- Plant
- Resource investigator
- Shaper
- Specialist
- Team worker

The internet is littered with tests to establish who is best suited to which role.

You will note that none of the preceding steps involve students critiquing other individuals in the group. This is because it is important to establish the principles before the specifics. Now is the time to do so. Before asking students to complete the group-work preference sheet that follows, make the ground rules clear. Comments such as those below are appropriate because, if negative, the writer takes responsibility for their part in the interaction rather than blaming the other for their behaviour or personality and, if positive, they focus on skills and qualities rather than personality.

- I would like to work with Herbertas because he is very creative.
- I do not want to work with Kayleigh because she is my mate and we find it hard to concentrate when we work together.
- I would like to work with Asha because she is good at helping people compromise.
- I do not want to work with Lee because I find his lack of focus irritating.

Note that the first bullet point allows you to assess the extent to which students have understood the previous steps – again, a useful indicator when putting together performance groups. Also, to avoid the resentment that comes from a token consultation exercise, make it clear that, while not all their preferences can be accommodated, at least one will be.

You may feel that your rehearsal time is so limited that indulging in such exercises and activities cannot be accommodated. Surely your priority is to get them working? Eventually, yes, but if you do not spend time on this preparation your students will not use their rehearsal time effectively.

Group-work Preference

High-quality devised theatre is underpinned by effective group work. List five of the skills or personality types that you think are needed to create an effective rehearsal group.

1. _____

2. _____

3. _____

4. _____

5. _____

Bearing in mind your own strengths and weaknesses, state one person with whom you think you can work productively and one person with whom you think you cannot work productively. Your comments should focus on:

- Their skills and qualities rather than their personality.
- How working/not working with the people you name would improve your work and increase your skills in drama.

 I would benefit from working with _____
 because _____
 I would not benefit from working with _____
 because _____

Bearing in mind your own strengths and weaknesses, state one person that would benefit from working with you and one person that would not benefit from you.

_____ would benefit from working with
me because _____
_____ would not benefit from working
with me because _____

Elsewhere, I will suggest that you audit your Key Stage 3 curriculum and GCSE schemes of work for opportunities for extended rehearsals. It might also be worth a separate audit to establish where there are opportunities for your students to develop their self-awareness and their understanding of the group dynamic, and how these opportunities might be extended, not just in the Drama curriculum but also in other subject areas. Unless, of course, your students are already self-aware and understand group dynamics.

I wrote earlier that once you have the group dynamic right, other considerations fall into place. The debate regarding friendship or assigned groups has been covered. Now for those subsidiary questions.

Some people argue that mixed-ability groups lower the attainment of the high attainers rather than raise the attainment of the less able and that groups should combine like with like. Surely it depends on what we mean by 'high ability'? We all know the 'low ability' student who shines in Drama in a way that they do not in other subjects. I find it far more useful to think of *different* abilities. Some students may be more confident or charismatic performers than others, but they are often inclined to thrive in the limelight and sulk outside it. Frequently, they do not attain the marks expected especially in combination with other such students, precisely because they lack skills in shaping the material or interest in anything other than opportunities to emote. (See the answer to Question 13 for further information.) They need to be grouped with those who understand the medium and elements of Drama, as well as those who understand the importance of revisiting and reworking scenes and can persuade others to do so! It is not an exam that merely assesses acting talent: it is an exam that assesses understanding of how to create an effective piece of theatre. That requires a whole range of skills. And you can teach those skills. The process that has got you to this stage will give students a deeper understanding of their various strengths and weaknesses and how everyone, regardless of previous perceptions of ability, makes a positive contribution to the process and so to the final product.

The uncooperative, reluctant participant is discussed at some length elsewhere. In my experience, those who present in this way do not feel secure and need to be enlisted and encouraged. Assigning them a group where they can be is the first step. How to include the erratic attender is dealt with in answer to Question 7.

A few final points:

- Please do not feel that you must assign final performance groups at the start of the rehearsal process. In Part 2: Making, Structure 8: Same Starting Point, Different Outcomes outlines a process – as its title suggests – which uses the same stimulus for the whole class as the starting point. This allows you to experiment with various combinations of students, while also amassing material for possible inclusion, before making final decisions.

- How we function is affected by how we feel. And how we feel varies. It is also the case that our ability to show our strengths varies, depending on mood, circumstances and who we are working in combination with. So a group, however well selected in theory, can move backwards and forwards in those Tuckman phases. This is only to be expected. It is not a disaster. As your groups begin to understand and accept that the rehearsal process is about experimentation and discovery, rather than getting it right first time, they will realise that stumbling or taking a wrong turn is part of the process and that, sometimes, we have to go backward before we can go further forward.

- Often, when I am running a workshop, the teacher's feedback is that one of the most useful outcomes is that it has enabled them to step back and observe the group, with a different insight into the group dynamic and individual strengths and weaknesses. I mention this because, if we are self-aware, we know the powerful effect, positive or negative, that particular students may have on us. It is easy to get locked in to perceiving an individual or a group in a particular way. In assigning groups, it is vital to step back to look at what they do, not what they do to you! If you have a colleague who can come in to look at individual behaviour and group dynamics, as part of the process of assigning groups, it can provide the same, invaluable shift in perspective. They do not have to be a Drama specialist. Just observant.

2. How do I manage and monitor several groups rehearsing simultaneously?

This is the central question. The purpose of this whole book is to answer it. The structures in Part 2 will support the management and monitoring required. Therefore this answer concerns only the general principles upon which you build those specific structures.

In the answer to Question 1, I referred to the skills required to manage the group dynamics as combining firefighting and arbitration. If you have managed an extended devising process before, you'll probably have found yourself acting as a bizarre combination of nursemaid and sergeant major: cajoling, persuading, reassuring, bullying, demanding as required. I always liken the process to spinning plates. You will have your own simile. The point, as I suggested in the introduction, is that it is a tricky, demanding, exhausting and challenging task. Everyone finds it so, whether or not they admit it. It's not just you!

The key to managing and monitoring several groups simultaneously is *structure*. Structure the groups as outlined in the answer to the previous question. Structure the devising process using the three stages outlined in the overview at the start of Part 2: Making. Also, don't forget what you already know and what you already do! What are your normal class-control methods and strategies when they're working in groups? I make that point and I ask that question because I have seen teachers during the devising rehearsal process doing – or, more accurately, not doing – things that they would never dream of doing in an ordinary lesson. I wonder if contemplating the mountain climb that is managing the process is what causes some teachers to forget what they know about effective classroom management, as well as to jettison common sense? I am not suggesting that *you* would dream of leaving them to get on with it while you catch up with your marking or check your Facebook page, but it has been known. What message does that send to those students and what modelling does that provide? It's just not effective teaching.

Of course, the content of each rehearsal session will vary depending on the length of that lesson. Of course, the amount of effective work that gets done will vary, depending on the time of day and the point in the week that the lesson takes place. However, whatever stage you are at in the overall devising process, the basic principles – and structure – for each rehearsal session remain the same as for other Drama lessons:

- An introductory activity. Beginnings are tricky, whether it's the opening of the play or the opening of a lesson. Students will be coming from different classes with news to catch up on. Get them focused and on their feet as soon as possible. Otherwise they will talk for hours. Part 3 of this book is packed with exercises that can be used as a whole-group warm-up, a focusing exercise, an activity that models something which should be incorporated into their work.

- A specific task for each group, tailored to their needs at this stage of the rehearsal process. Each structure in Part 2: Making features a sequence of such tasks, designed to be used as the main activity in each lesson. Different groups require different things: that's why there are ten structures to choose from. I always assign this task in writing. It saves time, ultimately. They can all start promptly. They have the brief written down so, if they weren't paying attention to your verbal instructions – which has been known, after all – it is there as an aide-memoire. You can check and clarify as required as you move from group to group, guiding and intervening as required. (At certain points, with certain groups, the task may merely be just getting on with it!)

- A concluding activity. This should involve showing work in progress. Showing of work in progress, whether to another group, to the teacher or to the whole class, is a vital part of the process. That's why it's built into all the structures outlined in Part 2: Making. (Why it's so important is explained in that part's introductory overview.) A little pressure is a good thing: knowing that their work will be shown encourages most students to make more effective use of their precious time.

- Some exam specifications require you to assess the process and for students to evaluate the process. Some do not. Regardless of whether there is a formal requirement to do so, reflection and evaluation should be built into every session, in order that the group can identify what has been achieved and what they need to work on next. (Again, this is discussed in more detail in the overview at the start of Part 2: Making.)

- So, in summary, the session-by-session lesson planning outlined above and the methodology outlined in the structures in Part 2 should result in an active, dynamic, manageable rehearsal process without you feeling like it's one long white-knuckle ride.

A few general principles to conclude, learnt by me through bitter experience:

- The more preparation you do, the more time you have in the lesson to troubleshoot, to observe individual group dynamics, to work with specific groups – in fact, to manage and to monitor the devising rehearsal process.

- Make sure every group records every single thing they do. They can write it down, they can record it, they can film it (or you can), they can photograph it, they can draw it. But keep a record they must – and they and you must know where those records are kept. It's staggering how much time a group can waste trying to remember and reconstruct what they did only yesterday, if they have assumed they will remember it. They won't. They don't. They'll need it to develop their work and, if the process is assessed, you'll all need the information as evidence for assessment.

- There has to come a point when you need each group for an hour or two on their own without any noise from other groups. Book extra rehearsals with groups at lunchtime or after school early on in the process. Sell the benefits of your undivided attention as a positive luxury! *Never* sell out-of-hours rehearsal as a detention.

- Finally, managing and monitoring the rehearsal process becomes a far less fraught process if your students have prior knowledge and experience of the specific skills required. The answer to the next question suggests ways of auditing your overall curriculum to ensure that they do.

3. The group I am teaching has very low-level skills and very little ability to work productively for any length of time. How do I raise them to the required standard?

Low-level skills are one thing. The inability to work productively for any length of time is another. The two issues may or may not be connected. I have encountered plenty of students with high-level individual performance skills whose attainment is limited by their inability to work productively for any length of time.

Let's solve the present problem: your current exam class. Then let's look at longer-term strategies and solutions in order that the question you pose does not crop up again and again, year after year. The appropriate response to your problem depends on various factors. The most important of these factors is the class's previous experience. If, as discussed in answer to Question 1, the class has had a disrupted or unsatisfactory experience, they will be in a state of barely concealed panic, even if it does not present in that way. Inevitably, if your students have experienced multiple Drama teachers in the last few terms or years, they will lack both skills and confidence. This will lead to a reluctance to engage in practical work. They want to succeed but fear failure. The best way to avoid failure is to not try. It is crucial that this behaviour is recognised as being due to this and is not caused by hostility to the subject or the teacher. I know it feels personal. It isn't.

This brings us to the question: what skills do they have, however low the level? Are they better at some things than others? You'll already have started to identify their basic skills if you've used the relevant exercise in the answer to Question 1. Next, map those skills against the exam-board assessment criteria, to give you a sense of where the most significant gaps occur. If you browse the activities in Part 2 and the exercises in Part 3, you'll see I specify what skills each activity is designed to develop. Use whichever of those exercises and activities are appropriate to compensate for a skills gap.

If the class lacks the confidence to engage in practical work, it can be hard to identify what skills they lack. In which case I recommend you set a series of short, simple tasks with specific criteria. Further information on the use of criterion exercises is contained in the introductory overview to Part 2: Making.

Once you've determined what they can and can't do, you'll be in a better position to know quite what degree of crisis intervention is required. The lower the level of skills, the greater the need for a framework and for short, structured, guided activities and constant support and intervention. You may need to consider scripted work (see Question 9), if that's an option. You should certainly look at which of the structures in Part 2 offer the most scaffolding: Transgressive Love, Reportage, No Inspiration Required and The Third Way were all developed with and for groups who lacked skills and confidence.

Also, effort does not equal attainment. While recognising this fact, we must also acknowledge that the confidence to engage – to make the effort – is a necessary first step. Effort can, should and must be praised and rewarded. Lavishly.

That deals with the immediate problem. Now for longer-term solutions. If the model for most lessons prior to their devising rehearsal process has been to get into a group and do a play, show it, forget it and move on, then they are unlikely to be able to shift the way they conceive of rehearsing. They have not been trained. It's the difference between sprinting and long-distance running. Even if they *do* understand the concept of developing work over several lessons, it does not follow that they can or should be expected just to pick up where they left off at the start of the next lesson.

That's just one example. What else do next year's cohort need to know and be able to do, to raise their level of skills and make managing the process less stressful? To answer this question, there is a need to audit your overall curriculum to see to what extent candidates have acquired the appropriate knowledge, skills and understanding when they begin an extended rehearsal process.

When reviewing your schemes of work, ask yourself the following questions:

- Are there opportunities for increasingly long and independent rehearsal processes in preparation for the devised theatre requirements of your exam specification?

- Are there opportunities to develop an understanding that process has worth in and of itself, and that rehearsal involves experimentation and discovery, not just getting it right first time and moving on?

- Are there exercises and activities that enable students to develop understanding of different approaches to characterisation, including how such concepts as status inform characterisation?

- Are there exercises and activities that analyse dramatic structure, in particular what makes an effective beginning for a piece and how to sustain the audience's attention?

- Are there exercises and activities that will enable students to understand that revealing through action is more dramatically effective than telling through speech?

- What opportunities do students have to see theatre (whether these are trips to the theatre, visiting theatre companies or GCSE/A-level/BTEC work by older or other students)?

- What opportunities do students have to perform, whether to other classes or to other audiences?

- What opportunities do students have to understand the conventions of various theatrical genres and apply these to their own practical work?

- Generally, teachers stress the responsibilities of the audience: to be attentive and supportive. At what point do students become aware that the performer has responsibilities too? (Such as audibility, configuration of space, performance energy and commitment.)

> • What opportunities are there for students to recognise and demonstrate their understanding of the medium and elements of Drama within their work, and how these can assist and clarify dramatic form?

The following exercise is also useful for you, to help you ensure that your students do not begin a devising rehearsal process unaware of the specific demands of making theatre.

Plan three activities, one for Year 7, one for Year 8 and one for Year 9, in each of the following areas:

- Form and structure of dramatic performance.
- Cultural and historical understanding of different styles and genres.
- Reworking and refining work in rehearsal.
- Voice and language.
- Characterisation.

The activities should enable your students first, to understand and then, to revisit and consolidate each area, deepening and broadening their knowledge, skills and understanding each time.

4. How long should the rehearsal process be?

In post-show Q&A sessions, students – and sometimes teachers – marvel when they hear that the play took three or four weeks from first readthrough to opening night. However, directing a play, with professional actors, in a rehearsal studio, then – supported by technicians – moving into a theatre, is a breeze compared with the task of coordinating and overseeing however many groups of students devising pieces of theatre simultaneously. I've done – and do – both. I know which is easier! Apart from the fact that the play exists in the first place, a cast can and do rehearse all day every day, five or six days a week. Professional actors are used to learning lines and expect to spend time preparing outside of rehearsals. You have to cope with and factor in all sorts of conflicting demands on your students' time and attention. No one expects professional actors to revise for other exams at the same time, meet deadlines for other coursework assignments, cope with the stresses and strains of being a teenager, or the specific anxieties of big things riding on the successful outcome of their exam results.

Any and every rehearsal process requires pre-planning. This continues our theme of the need for structure. You need a timeline. If this seems obvious to you, good. In which case, excuse the next paragraph or so. You would be surprised at the number of teachers to whom it doesn't occur.

Establish the date of performance, then work backwards to determine when your starting point for rehearsals should be. I realise that negotiating a precise date for an external examiner's visit can be complex and that, sometimes, they can't do your preferred date. But you can certainly narrow it down to within a day or so. This will suffice for timelining purposes at the start of the process. If the performance is assessed by you (before your marks are externally moderated), pretend it's not. Pretend the date is set in stone and that you'll have your house repossessed or be evicted from your flat if you postpone it. A deadline concentrates the mind – or the minds of your students – wonderfully.

Once you know your exam date, decide how long before then they should be ready to show, but also in what way. A formal, public dress-rehearsal-style performance? A public showing of a five-minute extract of work in progress? I write 'public' because they will be showing work in progress within the class throughout the process, or at least they will if you are following my advice and using the structures in Part 2.

How far back from the date of that public showing does basic structure of their piece need to be in place? If there are lines to be learned, when, within the process, do you want them off-book? (Set that deadline at least a week before it's actually and absolutely necessary.) And so on, back to when you start, plotting in any milestones along the way.

As for when you start and how much time you should allocate: what does the information from your exam board suggest regarding the number of hours or weeks the preparation process should take? Use this as guidance, but not as gospel. You may need more time. You probably won't need less, unless you have an exceptional group. How long are your lessons? If you have been allocated single periods (or lessons of an hour or less), you may need a longer period overall because, by the time you've started and finished, there is not a huge amount of time in the middle of a single period for actual rehearsal. As suggested elsewhere, the time of day will also have an impact on productivity: if the luck of the draw is that all your lessons fall at the end of the day, allow a longer rehearsal period than if you have them bright and early.

It is also useful to look at the percentage of marks that are awarded for this part of your exam course. If, for instance, it's a terminal exam worth forty per cent, does this mean that two terms of a five-term course should be devoted to the exam? This formula may be slightly over-mechanistic but it's not entirely inappropriate. However, bear in mind that preparation for that forty per cent includes previous work in your Drama curriculum that develops the necessary skills. Some of that work can and does take place in other units of the course, before your formal devising rehearsal process properly begins.

All these things should also be considered and factored in to your rehearsal planning. Schedule in after-school rehearsals and any weekend rehearsals well in advance, so you can get parental permissions, if required, but also so you can avoid that atmosphere of panic and crisis intervention. You don't need to decide who is rehearsing with you when. They just have to know that they may be called for rehearsal.

What other exams are taking place that might have implications for your lesson-time rehearsals? It's never a pleasant surprise to discover that half the class will be missing from two lessons for an Art exam, while a handful are missing from the next for a module of Maths. Conversely, which of your colleagues do you need to make sure knows about the importance of rehearsal lessons? Make sure they know. At least three times. In writing.

However long the overall process, different groups will work at different paces. The structures in Part 2 and the exercises in Part 3 should enable you to ensure that they all are ready to perform at the same time. It is possible, though not likely, that some groups will peak too soon. It is more likely that you will have the type of group who don't know when something works and will want to tweak their work constantly. They want to improve it but end up diminishing it by unnecessary embellishment. If you have a group in danger of either of the above, schedule them to watch and advise another group for a session or two. Explain why. They will be flattered at the idea that their opinions and comments will be valuable and useful to another group – and they will be.

5. How do I enable students to avoid shallow, clichéd work?

Despite occasional appearances to the contrary, no one actively wants to produce poor work. So, to answer this question, we need to consider why some students do so. Put simply, when this occurs, it is usually because they don't know what constitutes good work. They don't know any better. Here are some questions for you to consider to ensure they do.

What have your students seen that models good work for them?

It's a statement of the obvious that Drama students should have access to as much high-quality theatre, in a range of styles and genres, as possible. This can be tricky: the cost of theatre-going, the amount of form-filling involved in the organisation of a trip, the distance to the nearest theatre and the quality of what that theatre stages all have an effect. Regardless of how much theatre your students see, they should certainly be shown devised performances from the previous year: as much can be learned from watching pieces that did not attain high marks as from watching those that did.

What do they fall back on?

Most of your students will get their idea of what constitutes acting and storyline from watching TV soap operas, romcoms or a range of action-packed blockbusters. At the time of writing, the *Twilight* series is spawning a lot of work about sensitive vampires. The trouble is that TV and film do not draw attention to the medium (the form), whereas devised theatre is assessed on both content and form and how the two come together. The student resource sheets, Making Theatre: Getting Started (page 148) and Depth and Detail (page 150) should help students understand that they need to consider both, simultaneously.

Do they know what is required?

I know this seems like a stupid question. However, you would be amazed how often when I'm visiting schools, observing work in progress, I am met with blank stares when I ask, 'What do you need to demonstrate in your work, to access high marks?' To what extent do your students understand the assessment criteria against which they are judged? And – because it should follow but doesn't, necessarily – are they applying that theoretical understanding to their practical work?

Do they have experience of rehearsing and developing work in depth?

See the answer to Question 3.

Have they done their research?

In my time as an examiner, I have seen pieces that told me that the Battle of the Somme took place in World War Two (and, given the soundtrack, that 'White Cliffs of Dover' was written before 1916). I have seen desegregated classrooms in plays set in apartheid-era South Africa. I have seen a Victorian aristocrat tell a rival, 'Dude, you're gonna get mashed.' I have seen postmen delivering letters to medieval castles. I have seen Jewish or Muslim characters on their knees in prayer in a distinctly Christian way. I promise you, I am not exaggerating. I hope my point is clear: if the audience is to remain engaged in the world of the play, the actors need to have done the appropriate research – and so do you!

Have they forgotten what they know?

Often, when I'm asked to observe GCSE Drama work in progress, I find myself asking students why they have forgotten what they know – not about effective theatre (although that too, sometimes), but about how people behave. For example, why is a character knocking on the front door of their own home? Surely they would have a key? Why is someone saying, 'I'm really angry with you, right?' when they know that if their mum is angry, she slams the pans around, becomes monosyllabic, avoids eye contact and says she's fine? Students know a great deal about real, recognisable human behaviour, as well as how different people speak. Yet often, they seem to jettison that knowledge in their rehearsal process.

Do they understand the importance of the relationship between narrative and form?

Although, in answer to Question 11, I suggest that some storylines are best avoided, a lurid storyline is not necessarily a problem. *Oedipus*, *Hamlet* and *Medea* are not subtle stories. It's important to bear in mind that it's not the story you tell, it's the way that you tell it.

All of the above are things to look out for as you monitor work in progress, as well as checking for narrative clarity and economy, depth and detail of characterisation, the consistent and appropriate use of conventions, and whether they know why they're using them. (I think of this as the 'too many techniques too soon' trap.) All of the structures in Part 2: Making, and the three-stage model suggested there for the devised-theatre rehearsal process, should enable you to ensure that your students avoid shallow, clichéd work.

6. How do I ensure that boys engage and attain?

It's not just you and it's not just Drama. Statistics indicate that girls do better in GCSE Drama, but they also show that girls outperform boys in most other subjects too. Also, we must be wary of generalising and stereotyping. Some boys display none of the characteristics or types of behaviour discussed and described in this section. However, those probably aren't the boys that you are worried about!

Years back, when I was teaching in the East End of London, there was a unit of work on an elective mute. It was a whole-group role-play. Mantled as experts, the class were consultants, doctors, psychiatrists, specialists, all attempting to uncover what had occurred and to persuade the mute to speak. We were at the stage where a volunteer, in role, was asked to try various strategies to get the mute child to speak.

The volunteer in question – let us call him Dean – was one of those wiry, feisty, bantamweight hard nuts. In role, he was phenomenal. Without being prompted, his body language mirrored the mute's, his tone of voice was gentle, he asked open questions, he waited patiently for any sort of response, he read the body language signals superbly. He didn't succeed, but only because the student in role as the mute had been primed not to speak.

When asked to evaluate, Dean said: 'Well sir, *in role* (my emphasis), I felt frustrated because I couldn't get through to the patient. I felt very sorry for her, because I could sense her turmoil and pain. I felt judged and found wanting because I was aware that colleagues were observing me. I felt an oppressive sense of responsibility because I knew it was my task to break through and I couldn't do so.' Pause. Me: 'And how did you feel as yourself?' An instant shift in Dean's body language. 'It was alright.'

The point of this anecdote is that, for all sorts of reasons, most boys (and boyhood is a state of mind that lasts well beyond the teens) find it hard to acknowledge or articulate feelings, fear loss of face and do not like to appear vulnerable. This fundamental fact underpins the issues that lead to under-attainment. It is very hard to imagine the agony of being a teenage boy, particularly if you haven't been one. Even if you have been one, the pain, like that of childbirth, tends to fade. (Being a teenage girl is pretty hideous too in different ways, but you're not asking about them.) It's as well to try to keep this in mind, given that this state of being manifests in all sorts of ways which can be unhelpful both to the group and to the individual concerned, and wildly irritating to deal with.

Over the years, I've compiled a list, based on my own observations and the comments, complaints and insights of numerous Drama teachers, on the differences between how boys work and how girls work. I say 'differences' for two reasons.

- To formulate it as 'differences' rather than 'difficulties' reframes the issue.
- The differences may or may not be negative.

As an exercise, go through the following list. You may disagree with some statements. You may feel that some contradict others. You may have others to add in yourself. Whatever the case, in the right-hand column, put a tick if you think it's a positive attribute, a cross if it's a negative quality and a question mark if it could be either or if you're not sure.

Boys respond well to physical tasks.	
Boys prefer comedy, perhaps as a defence mechanism to avoid working in depth or revealing emotion.	
Boys are resistant to starting tasks.	
Boys' responses are raw or literal, whereas girls' responses are more considered.	
Girls discuss and plan for longer; boys stand up sooner.	
Boys take longer to settle.	
Boys get over conflict more quickly than girls. Boys don't hold grudges or, if they do, they mask the fact, as an acceptable social response.	
Boys' written work (and verbal evaluation) is weaker than girls'.	
Boys are more confident with physical work and more able to take risks.	
Boys like competition. They want to win, but don't want to lose face so may not participate through fear of failure.	
Boys love and need praise.	
Boys prefer an immediate response. They are not so good at deferred gratification – hence a sustained rehearsal period is inherently problematic.	
Boys are more delicate than girls with regard to criticism.	
Boys are worse at listening to instructions. (A statistic claims boys can't hold more than three instructions at one time.)	
Boys are not as good at abstract work.	
Boys cannot concentrate for as long as girls.	
Boys are better at performing aggressive emotions and at stage fighting.	
Boys are less enthusiastic readers: words equal work.	

By analysing the traits of male teenage behaviour in Drama, you will be able to play to their strengths and enable them to play to their own strengths too. Using strategies that utilise what you have identified as positive attributes, and strategies that minimise the effects of the negative attributes, will enable boys to engage and attain, regardless of whether the class you are working with is mixed or boys only.

What might those strategies be? In the report *Boys' Achievement in Secondary Schools* (July 2003), OFSTED found that: 'Boys often respond better to lessons that have a clear structure and a variety of activities, including practical and activity-based learning, applications to real-life situations and an element of fun and competition.'

In theory, this means that you are off to a head start as the effective Drama lesson features most of those points most of the time. Here are some of the other strategies that I, and others, have found work in enlisting boys and retaining their attention. (You will notice that many of them can be applied to the discouraged, unconfident groups of students of either gender discussed in answer to Question 3):

- Individual feedback works better than what is perceived as criticism in front of the group.
- Physical tasks with built-in controls.
- Time-controlled tasks with targets to achieve each lesson.
- Avoid a right-or-wrong-answer outcome, so they can't be wrong.
- Short, sharp activities, each building on the previous activity.
- Lots of praise.
- Stimuli which involve as little reading as possible.
- The 'drip-feeding principle' – introduce text gradually.
- When exploring an issue, work from the outside in to make an emotional connection.
- Start with what they know and can do, then lead them elsewhere.
- Select appropriate themes – with a 'safety net' so they are not obliged to reveal personal doubts and fears unless they want to.
- Challenge them to a sensible response: 'Some boys your age probably aren't mature enough to deal with the subject we're about to start.'

- Consider and assign groupings very carefully.
- Say 'No' but explain why. Use the exam specification and the assessment criteria as a buffer: 'Your impersonation of [insert current comedy god for teenagers] is hilarious but it won't get the marks that your talent deserves because . . .'

The structures in Part 2: Making embody many of these principles and strategies, and can be further adapted to include more. You will also notice that Structure 9: No Feeling, No Emotion is specifically designed for use with boys' groups. In addition, many of the exercises in Part 3: Refining, Troubleshooting and Finishing can be used as the type of short, sharp tasks mentioned above.

7. How do I include the erratic attender without jeopardising the work of the others?

This is the question that I'm asked more than any other – and with good reason. It's a major headache. It creates a problem for whatever targets you've been set for attainment. If you have twenty students in your group, a single candidate will count for five per cent of your overall pass rate. It creates a problem for whichever group to which the erratic attender is assigned. It also allows that group, if they are that way inclined, to create obstacles and to scapegoat, to use the erratic attender as the reason why they can't or shouldn't get on with the task. It can have an impact on their work: the erratic attender is, by definition, likely to be poorly prepared. They are easy for an examiner to spot: their work is more tentative, they tend to be looking towards the others in movement sequences, double-checking that they're doing the right thing at the right time. Their performance lacks commitment.

The problem can be minimised in two ways. The first is anticipation. The second is damage limitation: there are ways to ensure that their presence – well, their absence – does not jeopardise the overall attainment of the group.

First then, anticipation. Very few students start to attend erratically halfway through Year 11. It is likely to have been an issue already, well before the rehearsal process starts. The register for Year 10, whether yours or your predecessor's, will indicate who is likely to make the rehearsal process problematic for themselves and the others. The canny teacher will then alert everyone and anyone: parents and carers, form tutors, examination officers and senior management at the start of Year 11. Drama, uniquely, requires group work. A commitment to the rehearsal process is a vital part of that. This needs to be explained slowly and clearly, if necessary with diagrams. Appeal to the erratic attender's better nature: the team needs them. The cunning Drama teacher has even been known to suggest that the ultimate mark is determined not just by being there on the day but being there for every rehearsal. (In some cases, where an additional mark is awarded for contribution to process, this is actually the case.) Attendance should be monitored carefully and, if it helps, a contract signed so that the erratic attender is aware that, if her or his attendance doesn't improve, she or he will be withdrawn from the exam. Ask yourself: what percentage of lessons attended can you work with, if you have to?

It is difficult to get someone removed from an exam but possible, with sufficient warning and with the support of senior management. However, if the student is withdrawn, where will they go? If you are required to have the non-exam candidate in your classroom, what will they do, other than distract rehearsal groups? In which case, is it worth the effort of withdrawal? It may be, for one reason or another, that you're stuck with them. In which case, we move on to damage limitation.

If you've read the answer to Question 2, you'll know I recommend that you spread out the erratic attenders. That had probably occurred to you anyway. A group, although they will grumble and complain about having to work with an erratic attender, can contain one, as long as certain things, outlined below, are in place. A group with two is asking for double the amount of trouble. Nevertheless, it is an issue for the others in the group, so don't bullshit them. Reassure them. Explain to them how the process, the stimulus assigned and the structure will enable them to succeed even with a part-time attender. Flatter them. Explain that the reluctant attender's performance will be enhanced by working with such able students and that it doesn't have to affect the group's performance.

If you read through the various structures in Part 2, you will see which ones can best accommodate the erratic attender. You might choose a multiple narrative. Then, if necessary, their role can be removed. A 'messenger' role or a lone monologue – with another student in the group on standby to step in – will enable the erratic attender to get a mark, however low, for the performance. In the process, the principle of assigning tasks and targets for each lesson/rehearsal on a session-by-session basis (see Part 2) enables you to set work which does not require the erratic attender to be present. In this way, it is easy to avoid 'We can't do any work because X is not here.'

Finally, when the student in question is there, try not to give them a hard time, however irritating you find them and however worn down you are by the constant grumbles from the group. If they don't enjoy coming, for whatever reason, it is counterproductive to do so. If a student is greeted with 'Thank you for gracing us with your presence' or similar sarcasm, it's not going to make them feel better about you, school, or themself. Give them lots of support and encouragement, even if you have to grit your teeth to do so. Make them feel good about their group and the way their work is developing.

8. What degree of directing and guidance is appropriate?

Whatever degree is required to enable your students to get the highest marks possible. You have, I trust, been directing and guiding your students for some length of time. That is, after all, the role of the teacher. So why stop now?

I have known teachers who have misunderstood the requirements of this part of the exam. They don't want to cheat. They don't want their students penalised for getting additional help. But they will not be, as close reading of whatever exam specification you follow will reveal. The guidance provided by the exam board, the overall report on the exam last year and the specific report on your centre's work the previous year will provide invaluable clues and guidance. And reassurance. An exam board recognises that high-quality work emerges from well-structured preparation. An exam board understands that students need support, constructive feedback, monitoring and advice.

The historical metaphor for learning – children as empty pitchers waiting to be filled with knowledge – has never been much use in arts education which, rightly, involves developing creativity and self-expression. As a parent as well as a teacher, I realise that people need to be given responsibility and independence. However, if there is no framework, no mentoring, no possibility that arts practitioners might have knowledge and skills to impart, then we are back to an incoherent model of child-centred education. We are back to the teacher I mentioned in the introduction, assuming that his students would somehow manifest the skills they required.

Sometimes a teacher doubts that the students will be willing to accept their authority, in the form of their suggestions. That's irritating, of course, but that's where the assessment criteria can be used. Next time a student says, 'You're ruining our idea, miss,' show them the assessment criteria and point out that this is not a stand-off between them and you. You are merely interpreting the criteria for them and explaining what they need to do to attain the highest possible marks. It's not your opinion. It's the opinion of the exam board.

You are allowed to know more about what makes effective theatre, even if your students doubt that you do. And you are allowed to say 'No'. The better Drama teachers that I know ban certain topics and conventions from the start of Year 7. No gangs. No guns. No drugs. No car chases. No mimed cups of tea, cigarettes, fingers extended to indicate mobile phones. No knocking on imaginary doors while stamping the foot. No talk-show formats. No *EastEnders* or *Hollyoaks*-style exposition. Ban whatever you think will get in the way of them actually thinking about how they use space, or how best to communicate a narrative or theme to an audience. The earlier they internalise such things, the easier your life will be when it comes to an extended devising process.

Be wary, though, of imposing too rigid a house style. A house style can be a good thing but there is some evidence that, while it can raise the mark of less able students, it can also limit the mark of the more able. I've seen slick pieces with no ownership. Like so many dressage ponies, the students have been drilled to within an inch of their lives. You can see the fear in their eyes. The structures in Part 2 provide an appropriate balance between the need to structure, guide and direct, and the need for students to contribute to the creative process.

If you want to check that you're getting that balance right, the question to ask is 'Why?' 'Why is your character saying (or not saying) this?' 'Why that movement sequence?' If they don't know the answer, they are just following orders, either from you or from a fellow student: a dominant personality can lead to a lack of ownership for the other students in that group, too. However, bear in mind that a student may know why they are doing something but struggle to express why. Many actors (professional and student) struggle to articulate such things. So it may need facilitation, in the same way that reflection and evaluation often require careful questioning. Bear in mind too, that just because a student can explain fluently why they are doing something, that does not mean that it's working. Intention does not equal effect!

9. To what extent is it appropriate to use existing scripts, and do these benefit or limit candidates' attainment?

Entirely appropriate at all levels, if your exam board offers scripted work as an alternative to devised work, but – given that this is a book about devising and the devising process – rather beyond its scope! However, since you've asked, here are a few general points.

If there is a choice, I tend to recommend devised work in preference to scripted work. In my experience and observation, it is easier for devised work to attain higher marks. After all, it is a very specific skill to be able to take lines written five years, fifty years or five hundred years ago; memorise them, then make them sound as if they are occurring to you right now, this minute. It is not a skill that is usually facilitated in Key Stage 3 or Key Stage 4 Drama where the emphasis tends to be on improvisation.

Memory is a muscle: the more it is exercised, the better it gets. If your students are not used to memorising or rote learning, assigning them a script may be setting them up to fail. A scripted piece is only as good as the weakest member of the cast's ability to retain lines. You'll know this if you've ever acted with someone who doesn't know theirs. Devised pieces, on the other hand, have the capacity to raise the less able candidates to the level of the highest. In the answer to Question 3, I mention the specific challenges you face if you have taken over a group who lack skills. Sometimes, an appropriate script is the best way to ensure that they produce something – anything – that meets the assessment criteria at an appropriate level. Bear in mind, though, that their lack of skills may extend to an inability (due to inexperience and lack of confidence) to learn lines. If this is the case, it's worth testing out the extent of the group's ability to memorise, before it matters – which is to say, before they are assessed. (It follows too that if you're considering scripted rather than devised work for a group you know well, then make sure they have had opportunities for rote learning throughout their secondary Drama curriculum.)

If you do opt for scripted work:

- Make sure your students know not just what they are saying but also why. It seems like an obvious point but I see far too many actors (and not just at school or college level) who have only an approximate rather than a specific understanding of what the words they are saying mean, and no apparent understanding of what impels them to speak.

- Build in a date for students to be 'off book' far earlier than you actually need them to be. And build running lines into their process. An actor, at any level, only really begins to be able to act when they no longer have the script in hand. Also, the first time a scene or an entire play is tried without scripts, be prepared for things to go backwards before they go forwards. It's like the first time a child rides a bicycle without safety wheels: wobbly, tentative, but a vital step on the road to fluency.

- Ensure that the students do off-text exercises, to provide sufficient depth and detail. Many of the exercises in Part 3:

Refining, Troubleshooting and Finishing can be used for these purposes.

- Of course, there is also a 'third way': a piece which combines scripted and devised material. If this seems an appropriate way forward for a particular group, have a look at Structure 8: The Third Way, in Part 2 of this book.

10. The exam specification we use stipulates a theme. Doesn't this limit what I can do?

No. On the contrary, it provides a framework within which to be creative. Of course, I would say that: as I wrote in the introduction, it is a fundamental principle of mine that boundaries provide a structure and a springboard. Narrowing down the available options helps. You wouldn't, I hope, begin a lesson without a starting point of some sort. That's really all that a theme is: it's a focus. In any case, no exam board is going to specify a theme that is not open to multiple interpretations. If you are doubtful, here's a sequence of exercises for you, rather than your students, to offer reassurance.

Pick one of the following themes (or use the actual theme that you have been assigned):

- Family
- Conflict
- Change

1. Brainstorm all the existing plays that you know which feature your chosen theme in some way. Do not be afraid of thinking laterally (for instance, does 'family' need to be biological relations?). Next, add any TV dramas, films, poems and novels on the same theme.

2. Go through today's newspaper. Make a list of any news reports and articles that touch upon your chosen theme.

3.   Review your schemes of work. Which units address the theme, however tenuous the connection?

4.   Look through Part 2 of this book. Which of the structures feature your chosen theme? If a structure doesn't, how might you adapt the stimulus or starting points to incorporate that theme?

Also, while it is the case that a theme will be elastic enough to incorporate most storylines, an assigned theme can be used as ammunition – if a battle is required – for any groups who want to go their own way and are unwilling to accept your expertise. Smile sweetly, point them in the direction of the theme and ask how their cliché-ridden idea about bank robbers, teen pregnancy, whatever, demonstrates the theme. (Of course, they may be able to, in which case, reserve your right to say 'No', regardless.)

Bear in mind that a theme does not relate exclusively to content, but also to form in general and aspects of the performance style in particular. 'Change' can perfectly well apply to any transformation of actor from character to character, or from scene to scene. Also bear in mind that you could usefully spend several sessions workshopping the given theme whilst you are considering your groups (see Structure 9: Same Starting Point, Different Outcomes in Part 2, for more suggestions as to how best to do this).

11. Should some subjects, themes and styles be avoided?

No. However, some subjects, themes and styles may be more appropriate than others. It depends on a group's ability to tackle and deliver that subject, theme or style. That's what will determine their level of attainment.

Before we go any further, it is necessary to define terms. The subject is the plot. It is not the theme. I always picture the plot as the vehicle that delivers the theme. The style is the manner in which a story is told and the conventions that are used to tell it. It follows, then, that style is related to the form (or genre) of the piece in the same way as plot is related to theme. As John Gielgud once remarked, 'Style is knowing what sort of play you are in.'

Some subjects are overdone. Whose heart has not sunk when a student says, 'We want to do a play about mental health (or abortion or child abuse)'? It is worth your students being made aware that, in an average season, an average examiner will typically see dozens of plays about child abuse, drug dealing or terminal illness. It's also useful to be aware what storylines have been gripping the avid soap viewer, if you don't watch them. You'd be surprised at the amount of plot plagiarism that occurs. I have seen some very effective and moving pieces set in asylums and (admittedly fewer) to do with child abuse. I have also seen work based on challenging and original themes where, for whatever reason, the students have not risen to the occasion. As has been mentioned elsewhere, it's not the story, it's the way you tell it. The relationship between content and form is what counts, as is demonstrated and reinforced throughout the structures in Part 2: Making.

If a group is desperate to tackle a particular subject, there is danger that they have worked out the plot in advance. This is never a good thing, as the section on avoiding pitfalls in the introductory overview to Part 2 explains. Here are some useful questions to ask the group in question, to determine whether you should agree that they do so.

- What aspect of the topic interests them? In my experience, it's usually less to do with the subject and more to do with opportunities it offers the students involved to over-emote.
- Can they handle this theme emotionally? Can they stay with it over an extended rehearsal period? Delving into a world of pain is draining and difficult but, if they are to achieve any degree of emotional connection and authenticity, they will need to be able to do so.
- What do they know about the subject and what insight do they have to offer? How will they avoid the banal or the sensationalist in their treatment of the theme?

On the subject of the banal, the average teenager suffers from a surplus of earnestness, as well as a tendency to believe that they are the first people ever to have thought of things which, to most of us, are perfectly obvious. You'd have thought that there are plenty of people who think that war or poverty are good things. Worse, some devised pieces seem to think that those in the audience are responsible for the evils of the world. Most audiences do not care to be hectored in an accusatory tone. For this reason, I steer students away from theatre-in-education because it tends to foreground the message or moral, rather than use the theatrical form creatively. If your exam board requires the group to identify a specific audience that's different, please ensure the group's attention is focused not only on what they want to communicate to an audience but also how they intend to do so.

As I said in answer to Question 8, it is perfectly legitimate to say 'No' to a subject or theme. Either for the reasons outlined above or because of where you work: for example, Satanism and witchcraft may not be considered appropriate topics in a church school. I also think you need to be aware of what values the piece communicates, overtly or implicitly. You would, I suspect, be startled if a group produced a piece that suggested that all gay men should be executed or that mosques or synagogues should be burned down. This does not mean that the effects of homophobia or racism are inappropriate themes or that homophobic or racist characters should not be depicted. Most gripping theatre involves conflict. It does mean, though, that the piece should not end up, unwittingly or consciously, endorsing the views of those characters.

Regardless of plot or theme, it seems harder to excel with some subjects and styles. Comedy is notoriously tricky. This is partly because what adolescent boys (and it tends to be boys) find hilarious may not tickle an examiner's funny bone. Their comedy tends to be at best derivative and, at worst, a straight steal from whatever is engaging the nation's youth. As someone who has directed several comedies, I know the success criterion is obvious: How often are they laughing? How loudly? That may not be an exam criterion as such, but it is surely part of how effectively a group is communicating.

There is also a general perception that non-naturalistic work gains higher marks. I am not convinced that what passes for naturalism actually is. Naturalism is an accurate and detailed representation of real life. It involves more than just having a fourth wall. It is far more than soap-opera-derived ranting and suffering. If your students have the skills to produce a true imitation of life, let them.

Theatre is a form that can explore, express and communicate anything. Two periods of time can exist simultaneously. Time can be slowed down – what else is a slow-motion sequence? – or accelerated. The play *The Royal Hunt of the Sun* famously contains the stage direction: 'They cross the Andes.' I myself directed a script that required us to stage the moment of a boiler-room explosion extended over a period of ten minutes, intercut with the Big Bang theory. Anything can be represented, but it cannot be represented literally, in the way that an action sequence packed with computer-generated special effects in a film does. This is where the fundamental connection between content and form comes in, as you will see throughout the structures in Part 2 of this book.

12. To what extent do costumes, set and lighting impress an examiner?

They don't, unless the use of them is being assessed – of which, more later. They impress students and that's the problem. In every class, there is bound to be a group who seem to think the primary purpose of their piece is to display as many costume changes as your average musical. It is always a giveaway when, if you ask about the theme or content or purpose of a scene, the response is: 'I thought in this scene my character would wear . . . ' If only they spent a quarter as much time on the content, form and precision of their piece.

As an examiner, too many costumes can be quite dizzying to contemplate. Is that the same candidate? Why have they changed costume? Are they playing a different character? Conversely, please make sure the examiner can distinguish candidates. You have no idea how hard it is to assess an ensemble piece if they are all dressed in basic, unadorned black, however striking and simple a solution it seems to be. All those girls in black leotards with their hair pulled back, like so many former Eastern bloc gymnasts.

Similarly, examiners do not want to watch pieces that are, in essence, about moving furniture. I like a sharply choreographed set change – for reasons discussed below – but if candidates want or need more than basic rehearsal blocks, and if they insist on moving those between every scene, they are failing to grasp what the exam requires. For, if the examiner is there to assess acting skills in relation to the understanding and communication of form and content (and a quick glance at the assessment criteria will confirm this), costumes, set and lighting have no bearing whatsoever on the marks awarded. Use this fact, particularly if a group is disinclined to accept your opinion or authority. Every time a group starts mithering about set and costumes, brandish the assessment criteria for the specification they use. Ask them to point out where the criteria mentions set or costume. They don't. If the group is concentrating on costume changes and set moving, then they're not thinking about the conventions they use for either transitions or for when a character is 'offstage'. If they're not considering these things they are losing the marks available for getting from one scene to another. (See Part 3: Refining, Troubleshooting and Finishing for useful exercises in relation to this.) For similar reasons, avoid the use of props, unless you're going down the route of extreme naturalism, and probably even then. Accurate miming counts as a consistent convention. Why spend time sourcing props when you could be gaining marks for not using them?

However, costumes – rather than costume changes – may well assist the student in making the imaginative leap into the world of the play. People move differently in formal outfits. Picture those formal occasions with specific dress codes: weddings, proms, a court appearance. A heavy jacket, a waistcoat and wing collar constrain and alter the way a boy moves, in the same way that a long skirt or a corset does a girl. Costumes can help create a character's physicality. Similarly, the wringing of an apron or the nervous adjustment of a tie can enhance the marks a candidate achieves for characterisation and movement. What supports and enhances the experience for the performer will inevitably do the same for the audience.

In the same way, sound can heighten the atmosphere for both performers and audience. We all have our favourite pieces. I recommend 'Some Christian Zeal and Activity' by John Adams or 'Alina' by Arvo Part

46

for instant poignancy. I've used 'Knee Play 1' (from *Einstein on the Beach* by Philip Glass) to enhance many a mechanistic movement sequence (it even features the dulcet tones of Laurie Anderson, counting!). I am probably responsible for the widespread use in East London of 'Angel' by Massive Attack for imbuing menace and suspense. Enhance the mood by all means. But be aware that it is easy for an examiner to tell the difference between music included to create an atmosphere that is lacking rather than music that enhances the mood that was there in the first place. Also, avoid too many sound cues unless you have plenty of time for technical rehearsals: a show is only as good as the sound operator, and if dialogue and music happen simultaneously, the latter should underscore rather than compete with the former. That's a balance that requires time and expertise to get right.

Lighting can enhance a piece too, but avoid mood lighting, especially for comedy. Comedy needs light. I don't know why but it's true. Why do you think sitcoms are brightly lit and stand-ups perform in a spotlight? I also urge you to avoid blackouts between scenes. I have already mentioned the marks that are available for transitions. Also, every time the lights go out, the energy and momentum of the piece halts. It has to be cranked up all over again at the start of the next scene. The piece should be conceived as a continuous flow, rather than as a certain number of scenes with gaps between them.

Of course, you may follow a specification where consideration and application of lighting, costume, sound and set are part of what is assessed. In which case, bear in mind my previous paragraphs. Or you may have candidates who are being assessed for their performance support skills. In which case, the key word is *support*. Their portfolio can and should demonstrate the possibilities they explored and discarded before choosing appropriate effects. Sometimes, students opt (or are opted) for such technical options because they lack the social skills to work with a group. Unfortunately, they need to be engaged in the process, because they need to know the purpose of a scene and the intended effect of a piece. This cannot happen if the student goes away, works by themselves, and returns with a high concept which is then thrown over the piece, like a blanket masking the identity of a high-profile prisoner on remand.

13. My best student last year did not get the marks they deserved. What happened? How do I avoid it this year?

To be brutally honest, they probably did. Often, I am asked to look at film of a performances that a teacher is convinced was under-marked. I make sure I do not know, before I watch, what mark was awarded. Nine times out of ten the mark I would have awarded is in line with the mark given by the actual external examiner.

The problem is that effort does not equal attainment. It is very easy for us to confuse the two, particularly when we know how hard a particular student has worked or what contribution they have made to the success of the process. Sadly, marks are not awarded for trying really hard nor – unless there is a mark for process – the input a candidate has made to the effective construction of the piece, or for working so diplomatically and supportively with the others – or any of the skills that make us appreciate and value a particular student.

You know what standards are within your centre. If you're also an examiner, you will have a broader picture. However, the question is how does the candidate stand in relation to all the other students taking the exam, around the country? Standards may shift, particularly when a new specification is introduced: it takes time for a common understanding of how the latest assessment criteria translate into levels of attainment to emerge. Certainly, at the time of writing, there is a justifiable furor about different students receiving different marks for GCSE English because they happened to sit the exam at different times of year. However, when I was an area leader, I moderated the marks of the examiners in my team, if necessary. My marks were moderated by an assistant chief examiner whose marks, in turn, were moderated by the chief examiner. So, in theory, procedures are in place to ensure that standards are in line with those across the country, whatever those standards might be. Having said that, miscarriages of justice do occur, from time to time. Mind you, in my experience, overmarking is as common as under-marking, so idiosyncratic marking or a rogue examiner are as likely to benefit candidates as disadvantage them.

You have the right to appeal a mark, of course, and sometimes marks are adjusted on appeal. But if you don't or if they are not, all you can usefully do is contemplate what might have happened. Consider the following questions:

- What clues does the examiner's report on your centre provide?
- What clues does the chief examiner's report provide on overall standards around the country? These reports usually include helpful bullet-pointed lists identifying the features of high- and low-scoring work.
- Did the work meet all the criteria? Even if by 'best student' you mean someone with exceptional acting ability, that in and of itself is not enough to ensure high marks because the exam assesses individual acting ability in relation to a collective understanding of form. It's a team effort, hence the emphasis I put on getting the groupings right elsewhere in this book.
- At what level did the work meet all the criteria? In the overview to Part 2, I write about how shallow use of form can limit attainment.
- If you have a house style, did that limit the marks of the more able candidates in the group? As mentioned in response to the question on directing and guiding, it can do so. Was there clear ownership of the performance?
- Was the performance too short or too long?

Ultimately, on the day, some students will exceed expectations and some will fail to deliver. I began writing this book during the London Olympics: not everyone who was expected to get a medal did so.

14. I worry that an inappropriate audience response will distract the visiting examiner or undermine the performers. What can I do to avoid this situation?

Firstly, do you need an audience? Is it required by the exam board? If not, then you might consider not having one. However, most assessment criteria include consideration of how well performers and piece communicate to an audience. This suggests that an audience comprising more than a visiting examiner and a couple of Drama teachers will benefit the work: every actor knows that a full house is preferable to a sparsely populated auditorium. In theory, an audience should raise your performers' game. In practice, it has been known for students to start playing to the gallery or become self-conscious. Both of these are to be avoided.

Secondly, what do we mean by an 'inappropriate response'? That's not a facetious question. We probably all agree that talking throughout a performance is socially unacceptable – in the theatre, at least. (Anyone who has been to a cinema recently may have been driven to distraction by murmured or louder conversation.) However, with my director's hat on, I have remonstrated with teachers who allowed their students to use mobile phones (with their distracting illumination) to make notes during a performance. I have also seen teachers 'sssh' their students when they laughed. During a comedy. Maybe there is less of a shared understanding than we think.

In general, there are three possible causes for an inappropriate response:

- The audience do not know how a theatre audience is expected to behave.
- The audience know how they are expected to behave but chose not to.
- The play being performed does not engage their attention, for whatever reason. In which case, snorts of derision and fidgeting, though harsh, may be appropriate.

So, to avoid the distraction and undermining that rightly concern you, you need to do everything possible to ensure that none of these factors come in to play.

Ironically, the most distracting members of an audience can be your own students, specifically those who have just performed or those who are about to do so, because they are the most distracted. And why would they not be? They need to time to prepare and they need time to wind down after a performance. Sitting in the audience is not the place to do either of these things. If you work alone, do your utmost to find a supportive colleague who can supervise students in a separate room immediately before and after their performance.

If the performance is public and you are not sure that family and friends know the expectations and conventions of theatre-going, then an examined performance is not the occasion to find out. You might consider a public dress rehearsal instead, but you need to ponder whether that is helpful. It can lead to an anticlimactic performance in front of the examiner. Also, everyone is a critic. A casual remark can lead to a performer losing faith in their work or comparing it unfavourably with other pieces. Neither of those is useful. It's probably safer to schedule a public performance after the examined one.

If you do have a public performance, before, during or after the examined one, bear the following points in mind:

- Stipulate a minimum age and enforce that vigorously. I don't have to tell you how distracting and irritating crying babies and wandering toddlers can be for performers and other audience members alike.

- Make sure you have sufficient help and support on the door. You have more than enough to do without incorporating front-of-house and ushering duties into your job description.

- Make it clear that everyone is there for the duration, not just for the piece that features his or her child, sibling or mate. Some coming and going between pieces is legitimate, but only for those who have performed and calmed down and those who need to go and prepare. But it needs to be managed and to happen discreetly.

- For me, the most appropriate audience to sit alongside an examiner are those in Year 10 if we're talking about GCSE or Year 12 if we're talking about A level. They are likely to be supportive

– and if there is any hint that they are not, you have the weight of the institution on your side. More importantly, it shows them what standards they should be aiming to achieve – or exceed.

- Your primary task, despite any private doubts and fears about a particular piece of work, is to get your students on stage with a sense of confidence and pride in their work. Regarding an audience, whatever and whoever are most likely to help sustain that confidence and pride throughout the performance is the choice you should make.

Part Two
MAKING

Overview

If the first part of this book lays the foundation, this part raises the building. Having prepared the ground for the devising process, Part 2: Making offers a range of structures within which your students can work effectively and produce performance work that is dynamic, powerful and attains the highest possible marks. Use of these structures enables you to manage and monitor the process with relative ease, identifying problems with the work that is in development before those problems become insurmountable.

Why are these structures necessary? Because, while managing the devising process can be tricky, the actual process of devising is even more so. When a script exists, form, narrative, genre and theme are given. The task is interpretative. In contrast, whatever the starting point for devised work may be, nothing is a given, beyond the need to develop and shape the material into something that engages an audience.

In essence, your task is to enable your students to demonstrate their understanding of content and form and how the two come together. In my experience, to facilitate this, it helps to recognise that a devising process involves three more or less distinct stages. These stages can be summarised as follows:

1. **Generating and Exploring** – Trying out different ideas and experimenting with different responses to whatever stimulus and starting points are provided. Developing a range of possibilities and directions for the second stage.

2. **Selecting, Structuring and Developing** – Wherein the theme becomes clear and the plot and the characters are shaped, as is the style and form of the piece.

3. **Rehearsing** – Revisiting and reworking the material, but also polishing the piece, honing and discarding as necessary, to ensure that what the performers wish to communicate to the audience is done with as much clarity, imagination and precision as possible. In my mind's eye, this stage is like rehearsing a new play: the structure and the content are there but some rewrites and showing of work in progress is required.

Elsewhere, I have suggested how long an overall rehearsal process should be and how to monitor and manage several groups working simultaneously. The structures that follow in this part, and the three-stage model outlined above, provide an overall shape and a framework for the process. Within this framework, individual lessons (which we must now think of as rehearsal sessions) still need to be planned and structured. (For further advice, see the answer to Question 2 in Part 1: Preparation.) As a rough rule of thumb, the ratio for the three stages of the devising process is 30:35:35. But boundaries can blur. Some groups generate a lot of possibilities in a relatively short time. Others move backwards and forwards between the selecting, structuring and developing required in Stage 2 and the polishing and refining of Stage 3.

This part of the book, Making, features ten structures, all arranged in the three-stage model. The premise for each is that a stimulus should be used to open up possibilities rather than close them down. There are various approaches: some begin with a theme, in others, a theme emerges from a range of possibilities. Some templates use specific stimulus material. Some offer ways of using a type of stimulus. Some provide frameworks while others are springboards. I make no apology for the fact that you will see some activities and exercises used in the first stage of more than one structure, although with variations in focus and emphasis. They are there because they produce the right results.

Different groups of students have different interests, needs and learning styles: in the introductory paragraphs to each of the structures I have suggested the particular types of students that might benefit from one template rather than another. You should feel free to mix and match the suggested activities and exercises, borrowing and substituting from one structure to another. You are the expert when it comes to your students: you know what will best enable them to generate and explore.

Use of these structures as well as the three-stage model should help to avoid the three major pitfalls I have seen that limit attainment.

The first potential pitfall is closing down the possibilities too early in the process. I cannot emphasise enough the dangers of working out the plot line in advance. It leads to shallow work and a failure to consider the relationship between subject and form. It is also a mistake to assume that the process of making theatre is a linear one. Ask any playwright! April de Angelis' play *Jumpy* began when she found herself writing a scene involving three characters and a gun. She did not know who they were or where they were at that stage. It follows, then, that it is also a mistake to establish the order of scenes too early in the rehearsal process. Of course, a good beginning is crucial. If the audience doesn't want to find out what happens next, there's a problem. But what makes the best beginning will not necessarily be clear from the start. Cast your mind back to your own essay-writing days: how often did the introduction in the first draft become the conclusion in the final version?

The following quote, from Paul Hunter, co-artistic director of Told by an Idiot, should be reproduced in large letters and displaying on the wall of every drama studio in the country:

Rehearsing is not about getting it right. That's the exact opposite of what it's for. I always say straight off, get up and try something. It's better. Because you may find something quite interesting that emerges in that stage. You often get people saying no to someone's idea before they've tried it. You say, 'Have you tried this?' 'No, no, that won't work.' Well, you don't know until you've tried it. It may be a brilliant idea. It might not be. But I always think you should try every idea. You've got to try it. And you can only know by doing it. You can't know by talking about it.

The second potential pitfall is the shallow use of form. As the previous point suggests, this is often because groups focus on the narrative without considering how the story is best told. However, it is mainly because they have a limited understanding of what is required. For instance, students often think the 'talk show' format is both a good and appropriate idea. It is neither, unless you think that the examiner's idea of a good time is watching an episode of Jeremy Kyle live on stage. Many pieces open at a moment of crisis or then flash back to a simpler place and time; the subsequent action reveals how we got there. That's better, but that's to do with structure rather than a deeper understanding of what form involves and what form may be most appropriate to the content. Similarly, in an otherwise naturalistic piece, a character may break the fourth wall and reveal to the audience what they cannot reveal to the other characters on stage. There is nothing inherently wrong with that but there is a need for students to understand that a convention needs a context. That context is an understanding of form, or genre, and the rules and conventions of that form. It is, to return to a point made in the first part of this book, an understanding of what style of play you are in. Students also need to understand that narrative structure involves more than flashback and a monologue or two. It involves such things as narrative economy, clarity, revealing through action and subtext rather than merely dialogue.

Content informs form and style. Whether or not they are aware that they are doing so, students start shaping the material generated as soon as they begin to make decisions about form and style. To avoid the pitfall of the shallow use of form, there are five key questions:

- **What's the story you want to tell?**

must always be considered in conjunction with

- **How do you want to tell it?**

Following close behind comes the question

- **Why do you want to tell it?**

because this leads, inevitably, to

- **What effect do you want to have on the audience?**

and

- **How will you create that effect?**

However you structure your devising process, you and your students should bear these key questions in mind throughout.

You will see that criterion exercises are used throughout the templates. Put simply, a criterion exercise means that you stipulate what should or should not be included in an exercise, a scene or the final piece. Stipulating such criteria does not impede creativity or imagination but, on the contrary, provides a framework and focus for creativity. Criterion exercises are used for different purposes at different points. In Stage 1, they are used to help develop a range of ways of presenting ideas. In Stage 2, they are used to galvanise understanding of the relationship between style, content and form. In Stage 3, they are used to tweak, refine and improve the work, with a particular emphasis on narrative precision and economy.

In the introduction to this book I used the metaphor of sculpting the material. Criterion exercises can provide the tools to do so – but they need to be the right tools! Teachers often stipulate the use of certain strategies: the monologue and the flashback mentioned above, for instance, or the use of thought-tracking or split focus. These can be hammers, when chisels are required. For instance, I once watched a GCSE Drama piece in rehearsal. The scene featured a beautician pedicuring a pampered rich woman. The girl playing the beautician made her subtext crystal clear. She said nothing critical but the tone of her monosyllabic responses to the wealthy woman's self-absorbed prattle, the difference between her expression when looking at her client and looking at the feet, the rhythm and punctuation of the activity (manicuring the feet) provided its own commentary. Yet, when I returned to the group later, the beautician stepped out of the action to deliver a monologue on how much she hated the client. Why? Because the teacher had told her to include 'thoughts aloud'. What was intended to improve the work diminished it.

The third potential pitfall is a lack of reflection and analysis throughout the process. Some exam specifications require that students evaluate the process in writing and record how it contributed to the development and realisation of the final piece. Even if your specification does not, reflection and evaluation should be built into the process. It improves the quality of the work. If students are assessed on their ability to communicate with an audience, they must surely strive for clarity about what effect each scene and the overall piece is intended to have on the audience. How can they do this if they are not reflecting, analysing and evaluating?

I have written earlier about how much time is lost with students vaguely and vainly trying to recall what they did in the last rehearsal session. It goes without saying that your students should record (in some form) the work that they do, in order that it can be revisited and developed. Do not let them fall into the trap of merely telling the story of the scene they have been working on. They also need to make notes on how and why they are doing it, in order that they can reflect on their work. Your exam board may provide a range of evaluative questions to assign but, essentially, the key questions are:

- Is what we have done working?
- What do we need to work on next?

Their answers to these questions – and your own answers and opinions – will help you assign appropriate tasks (with criteria attached) and targets.

Of course, it is not what they *say* they have done or think they have achieved that counts: it is what they are *seen* to have done. This is why the showing of work in progress is vital:

1.   It enables you to monitor the work.
2.   It raises the stakes for the group and enables them to monitor their work: an audience gives the performers a sense of whether something is working in a way that cannot be achieved by just running through the scene with their group.
3.   The external eye and feedback from others in the class helps to clarify whether the intended effect is being achieved and what needs to be done next.

To support you and your candidates, four student resource sheets have been provided (pages 147–150). These sheets can be downloaded from www.nickhernbooks.co.uk/Making-Theatre. It is never a good idea to bombard students with too much information too soon. So, two of the student resource sheets, 1: Creating a Character: Getting Started and 2: Making Theatre: Getting Started, as their titles suggest, are designed to be distributed before the start of Stage 2. Student resource sheets 3: Developing a Character in Depth and Detail and 4: Making Theatre: Tips and Pitfalls are designed to be used from the start of Stage 3. However, you know your students and what they need when so, really, you should use the student resource sheets at the points you consider most useful and appropriate.

The structures that follow each offer five activities in Stage 1. All of these explore the stimulus and generate material for Stage 2. Inevitably, the structures are more specific in their suggestions regarding this first part of the devising process because you know what scenes and possibilities have emerged from the first stage. I do not. Nevertheless, Stage 2 of each of the structures outlines specific points to consider in that stage of the process if you are using that structure. These points should be used within the framework of the five key questions listed on page 58.

Much of what you apply in the third stage will depend on where the second stage has got to. Again, you know where that is. I do not. So I can only make general points about what needs to be considered and monitored in the third stage. This overview for managing Stage 3 of the devising process has evolved through years of observation and experience of both what limits and raises attainment. On the subject of Stage 3, it can be hard – for them and for you – to see the wood for the trees. This is where the specific questions and exercises in Part 3 of this book, Refining, Troubleshooting and Finishing, come in. So, although I can't lead you from start to conclusion, I can provide you with a route plan. Good luck on the journey!

Transgressive Love

To attain high marks, candidates need to be able to create an effective narrative. This can be harder for some groups than others. A song lyric can be an excellent starting point for those who need a definite structure within which to create, but it needs to be the right sort of song. Songs that use images to paint pictures, that tell a story but which raise questions about that story: those are the ones that work, not ones that focus on feelings or emotions. To be useful in this context, the lyric should provide a narrative that describes an event (or series of events) but with an element of mystery: gaps that need to be explored and filled.

I've chosen 'Vrbana Bridge' by the American songwriter, Jill Sobule. It's a song based on a true story. Boško Brkić and Admira Ismić were in love: he was Muslim, she was Christian. They were shot as they attempted to cross the Vrbana Bridge, during the Siege of Sarajevo in the Bosnian conflict of the 1990s. The lyrics are reproduced below. The song itself can be downloaded from iTunes (as, apparently and increasingly, can anything ever recorded by anyone!). While there is a definite structure – a story with a beginning, middle and end – the theme emerges, as does the focus for the story. The theme, in this case, is the perennial one of transgressive love.

The tragic love story, whatever the transgression of social or religious codes and whether or not it involves the classic love triangle, has enduring appeal. There are plenty of songs on the same theme that can be used instead of 'Vrbana Bridge'. 'Matty Groves' and 'Long Black Veil' spring to mind. The first is a folk ballad, concerning the lady of the manor's seduction of one of her husband's farm workers. The second is about a man who goes to the gallows for a murder he did not commit because he does not wish to reveal his alibi – an affair with his best friend's wife. Type either title into any search engine and you will find the lyrics. Songs about poverty, or the effects of poverty can provide a powerful stimulus too, providing they meet the criteria outlined in the introductory paragraph: try 'The Ballad of Hollis Brown' by Bob Dylan or 'Fast Car' by Tracy Chapman. The activities in the first stage are designed to be applied to whichever lyric you choose.

Vrbana Bridge
by Jill Sobule and Robin Eaton

They stood by the window
And watched the old church
Burn for the second time.
The light from the fire
Made her glow like an angel
As she pulled him down and smiled.
They lay on the bed,
There were shouts all around
They could shut the whole war out.
With the squeak of the springs
And tomorrow's dreams
And the beating of their hearts.

He would lay his arms down for her.
She would forgive his brother's crime.
They would do anything
To make it past Vrbana Bridge.

Well he looked up to Jesus
And she looked to the east
Where the sun was soon to rise.
She asked for Allah's blessings
To keep them both alive.
They had friends in high places
Who could do them a favour,
Turn a blind eye.
They'd seen so much hate

And death every day,
'Let's just let those two walk by'.

They would lay their arms down for her.
They would forgive his brother's crime.
Just for one moment they would
Let them pass Vrbana Bridge.

Through a crack in the wall
Of a sandbagged building
The soldier saw them fall.
He said, 'If love was their only armour
It did no good at all.'
They lay for six days
In a final embrace.
They had shut the whole war out.
The soldier blames the other side
But even he has his doubts.

He would lay down his arms down for her
He would forgive his brother's crime
He would lay down his arms
To let them pass Vrbana Bridge.

1. Generating and Exploring

1. Read the lyrics and/or play the song.

Individually, without conferring with each other, ask students in the group to:

- Summarise the story the song tells in a sentence.
- Summarise their emotional response in a word or phrase.
- Comparison with other narratives of transgressive love is encouraged so also ask them to list other transgressive love

stories that they know and what social codes have been broken in each story.

These responses will be used later: the first to support narrative focus and clarity, the second to help determine the intended effect on the audience, and the third to open up comparisons and parallels later in the process.

Next, the group should create five still images that tell the story. They should select a line or phrase from the lyric as a caption for each image. This caption could be written and displayed, in which case the group need to decide the best way to incorporate this display. Or the line can be spoken by someone, who steps out of image to do so. Or, given that not every picture needs to feature all members of the group, someone who is not in that image could speak it. Or a single member of the group could be designated as narrator or observer, who remains outside the images. Regardless of which of these is chosen, the group should consider how they move from one image to another as part of the task.

The activity is a good starting point because:

- Selection of key moments underpins students' understanding of narrative structure as well as beginning to address the rhythm and momentum of a piece.
- Making decisions about how to move from one image to another helps them to begin to relate form to content.

2. As a whole group, ask students to brainstorm who the characters in the story might be. They should – and will – begin with the characters they have depicted in the previous exercise. Their list should include:

- Those referred to in the lyric.
- Those directly affected by the events described in the lyric.
- Those who might be observers or onlookers to the events described.

Subdivide the group into pairs (or a pair and a trio). Ask each pair to create a monologue for a witness to the events described. They should *not* use the words in the lyric.

One of each pair performs the monologue to the rest of the group.

The monologues will be returned to in Stage 2 where they have the potential to be:

- Used to develop characters within the narrative, as well as different perspectives on the story.
- Given to an irregular attender so that they have something to do in the piece without affecting the whole group.

3. Ask the group to compile a list of questions raised by the gaps in the narrative. In general, questions that begin with 'who', 'what', 'why' or 'how' will open up possibilities for exploration. They also raise issues to be addressed regarding:

- Motivation
- Explanation
- Interpretation

Research may be necessary or desirable, depending on which narrative of transgressive love you are using: as mentioned elsewhere, if scenes are set in different times, places and worlds, then the performers need to be aware of any differences in social conventions and vocabulary. In the case of the Vrbana Bridge incident, there is a famous Reuter's news report of the event available online, as well as photographs. If the group hasn't already, make sure that reporters and photographers are added to the list compiled in Activity 2.

On the basis of the questions raised, ask the group to create two two-person scenes – before, during or after the narrative of the story – which fill in some of those gaps by answering some of the questions that have been raised. The scenes should not last longer than a minute and a half. Use of this as a criterion will encourage both narrative economy and consideration of what the subtext is and how to communicate it.

Stress that parts should not be cast yet on the basis of this scene or, indeed, of any of the work in the first stage. This is because, at this point in the devising process, the group needs an overview rather than an investment in a particular character. If final casting is decided too early, it can lead to an imbalanced narrative because the question becomes 'Where are my performance opportunities?' rather than 'How does this character best serve our narrative?'

4. Ask the group to create two more two-person scenes. The scenes should feature different characters, on different sides of the divide. However, this time, the content of one must mirror the content of the other. This might lead to the dialogue between, for example, Boško and his father on one hand and Admira and her mother on the other being the same. It might involve the same movements or gestures. In either case, the group should consider the best way of moving from one scene to another, or cutting between the two.

5. Ask the group to create a three-minute version of the story, using the form and conventions of a particular genre. This opens up consideration of which style and form might best suit the content.

Of course, which genres you suggest depend on which they are familiar with. A soap opera, a news report or documentary or Greek tragedy are worth suggesting. However, don't be afraid to try out what appears to be counterintuitive. Common sense might dictate that, say, *commedia dell'arte* is not an appropriate form within which to tell the story. That does not mean it should not be applied, as an experiment. To paraphrase the Paul Hunter quote in the introduction to this section, who knows what might emerge?

2. Selecting, Structuring and Developing

The group now has a range of characters and, therefore, a range of perspectives on the central event. They also have various forms and conventions that may be explored, developed and used (or not!) in their final piece. They have scenes, speeches and sequences that might be developed or included in their current form.

Who plays which part (or parts) should emerge from this stage of the devising process. The group should also consider what resonances doubling might create:

- What if the same actor portrays both fathers, violently opposed to each other?
- What if the actor playing a neighbour who feels they have no responsibility to intervene also plays the sniper who kills the lovers as they cross Vrbana Bridge?

As mentioned earlier in this structure, the theme of transgressive love is perennially popular. The roots and reasons for this appeal are worth noting and discussing with students, as are other examples of 'star-crossed lovers'. They might choose to translocate the story to a different place and time, or create a piece that compares and contrasts it with another, similar narrative set elsewhere.

Many such narratives are structured with dramatic irony in mind, so that the audience is ahead of the characters. *Romeo and Juliet* is the classic example of this. We know that Juliet is not really dead, which affects how we view her parents and her nurse's reaction. We know that Friar Lawrence has sent a message to Romeo and we know what it tells him, even if he does not. However, we know the outcome from the very start because the Prologue tells us exactly what will happen to the protagonists. Is this a narrative structure that could and should be applied to the story of Boško Brkić and Admira Ismić?

I would also pose the following questions:

- What do they want the audience to feel? Pity and compassion for the protagonist (or protagonists), but, perhaps, an understanding of why there was opposition, or the impact of the relationship on others? This is the first question because what they want to communicate will inform their answers to the subsequent questions.
- Where do they start the story? Does it have to be chronological, as the lyric is, or do they wish to begin at a key moment and flashback? Do they want to use a recurrent image to return to, as a linking and framing device? This is where the images created in Activity 1 can come in handy as possible bases for either.
- What do they need to know? 'Know' covers both what they need to imagine and invent, to create characters of sufficient depth

and detail, but what facts they need to research about the world in which the event took place.

- Although they need to know, it doesn't necessarily mean that they need to show the audience. Therefore, what do they need to show? And, equally important, what do they *not* need to show? Is it a gap that will leave the audience floundering?

I would not, however, pose them all at once – too much information to process at the same time!

The student resource sheets (pages 147–150) will provide general guidance regarding:

- Creating characters with sufficient depth and detail: exercises regarding characterisation from Part 3: Refining, Troubleshooting and Finishing can also be assigned as part of this stage of the devising process, as required.
- Structuring and shaping the material in a way that will engage an audience's attention.

The group should also be aware that all decisions regarding content and sequence are provisional and may alter in the final stage!

3. Rehearsing

For general guidance on Stage 3 of the devising process, see pages 143–146.

Reportage

Reportage and oral testimony can make excellent stimulus material because they:

- Provide a framework and story with a beginning, middle and end to explore.
- Encourage empathy and understanding.
- Support depth and detail of characterisation (particularly of different modes of speech) and therefore attainment because the work is scaffold by research and by the inclusion of reportage and personal testimony.

Also, there is something about working on real events and real people that helps candidates to take their work seriously, should they find it difficult to do so.

The event you choose is best determined by the context within which you work, including location. There may be a local historical event that will particularly engage your students. Over the years, I have used or assigned various events, including:

The Penlee Lifeboat Disaster

On 19th December 1981, the voluntary crew of Mousehole, Cornwall, launched the lifeboat *Solomon Brown* in hurricane-force winds and battling against sixty-foot waves, in an attempt to rescue the crew of the cargo ship *Union Star*. Both ships and sixteen lives were lost.

The Guildford Four

A group of four young people were wrongly convicted in the United Kingdom in October 1975 for the Provisional IRA's Guildford pub bombing – which killed five people and injured sixty-five more – and imprisoned for over fifteen years. There was never any evidence that any of the four were involved with the IRA and all had alibis for the time of the explosion.

The Newham Anti-Terrorist Raid

In June 2006, Scotland Yard's anti-terrorist squad raided a house in Forest Gate, East London. Two hundred and fifty police officers were involved. Mohammed Abdul Kahar, one of the sons of the family whose house it was, was shot and wounded. He and Abdul Koyair, one of his brothers, were arrested, held and questioned for a week but released without charge. The event caused wide-scale outrage in the neighbourhood.

In the last few months, the publication of the Hillsborough enquiry or the joint-enterprise conviction of the young people involved in the murder of Sofyen Belamouadden at London's Victoria Station have offered great potential for powerful narratives. It is useful if there is an element of miscarriage of justice or social inequality because this will lead to exploration of appropriate forms and genres, as well as the social themes underpinning the story. Regardless of your starting point, you need a good summary of the event, which can easily be found on the internet: Wikipedia and the BBC websites are particularly useful, as is YouTube, especially for those who – like me – assimilate what we see and hear better than what we read.

1. Generating and Exploring

1. Ask the group to read the stimulus article (whatever that may be) aloud, one paragraph each. There is something about the act of collective reading, and hearing the event described which brings the account to life in a way that individual reading of it does not. Bear the earlier point about visual learners in mind too, when deciding the best form in which to present the stimulus material.

The group should then list questions in response to the article. These may be general ('How could this have happened?') or specific ('How must this, that or the other person have felt?'). Whatever the questions are, they will be useful as the basis of exploration through drama. They will also suggest the areas for further research, as well as providing a focus for deciding what they want their piece to communicate to an audience.

Next, ask the group to create an opening scene that will engage the audience and make them want to find out what happens next. This should be done with the proviso that the group (or you) might change their mind later in the process and agree a better opening. But it is always a good move to make the task (to create a piece of theatre that engages the audience's interest) explicit to our candidates.

2. Ask the group to create an abstract scene that explores and communicates a mood or emotion which the group feel is important in the material. The piece should focus on a character directly affected by the events described.

Stipulate that the piece should not last longer than one minute and should not involve naturalistic dialogue, although words and sounds are permissible. I would also impose another criterion perhaps that there should be five points of physical contact – no more, no less – between the performers as part of the sequence.

If the scene is shown to another group, or to the class as work in progress, and if they are asked, as per other structures (such as 3: Montage) to comment, these comments should be recorded. Not only do they indicate how clearly and effectively the performers are communicating what they intend to communicate, but the audience's interpretations may also open up other narrative possibilities and perspectives.

Music can heighten movement sequences but it can also narrow down responses. So, although the group should consider adding music to this sequence as and when they revisit it in Stage 2, silence is best at this stage.

3. Divide the group into pairs, or a pair and a trio. Each subgroup should create a monologue.

- One should be for someone directly affected by the events described, looking back on the event.
- One should be from a witness (or messenger) bringing news of the event shortly after it has happened.

By creating these contrasting monologues, the group begin to focus on both different perspectives and on the fact that, sometimes, a description of something shocking has greater impact than a depiction of the same event.

Research is not only permissible but also encouraged: the words of actual participants or witnesses can and should be included, if appropriate.

4. Next, ask the group to create a scene which focuses on a moment of choice for one of the characters directly involved in the event. This could involve a conscious decision to do or not do something. It might involve a decision which does not seem of any consequence at the time but subsequently turns out to be crucial.

Focusing on this moment of choice will help provide narrative structure in Stage 2 and emphasise the importance of key moments of climax or crisis.

5. Ask the group to consider what group of people might function as a chorus. By this I mean that they comment on events from a different point of view, rather than necessarily moving and speaking in unison. The chorus's perspective should be different from that of the protagonist. They may be indifferent or unaware. They may be wildly hostile to the protagonist(s). They may be any point in between. The group should decide on whether the chorus use direct address to the audience or whether they operate behind a fourth wall, interacting with each other, and confirming each other's opinions.

2. Selecting, Structuring and Developing

The group now has a range of characters and, therefore, a range of per-spectives on the central event. They also have various forms and conventions that may be explored, developed and used (or not) in their final piece. They have scenes, speeches and sequences that might be developed or included in their current form.

The student resource sheets (pages 147–150) will provide general guid-ance regarding:

- Creating characters with sufficient depth and detail: exercises regarding characterisation from Part 3: Refining, Troubleshooting and Finishing can also be assigned as part of this stage of the devising process, as required.
- Structuring and shaping the material in a way that will engage an audience's attention.

As this structure uses reportage, it is appropriate to use as many actual quotes from participants, observers and witnesses as possible. Addi-tional dialogue that they create should be informed by the vocabulary, rhythm and idioms of the real people involved.

There are any number of verbatim plays: it is worth assigning some of these for the group to read, to support their search for a suitable form and structure for the content. I recommend *Execution of Justice* (1984), by Emily Mann, a verbatim drama about the trial of Dan White, the man who shot Harvey Milk, because, although every word in it was spoken by a real person, the play moves backwards and forwards in time and in and out of the courtroom. The tribunal plays, commissioned by Nicholas Kent at the Tricycle Theatre and dramatised – which is to say edited from transcripts – by Richard Norton Taylor are another useful source. The best known of these is *The Colour of Justice* (1999), based on the transcripts of the Stephen Lawrence enquiry. However, be wary of merely appropriating the 'courtroom drama' format.

The following points also need to be made and considered:

- Why is it important that people (in this case, the audience) know about the event? What does it tell them about the world in which we live?

- Stress the importance of research to ensure historical accuracy: nothing jolts an examiner out of the piece like the anachronistic use of a mobile phone, a house which appears to feature electricity before it was invented or . . . you get the idea.

- Stress the change in perspective that time and hindsight bring: contemporaneous accounts of, for example, the conviction of the Guildford Four present a very different account from retrospective ones. This may well affect how the group structure their piece.

- What do they want the audience to feel? Pity and compassion for the protagonist (or protagonists), but, perhaps, an understanding of the impact of the event on others?

- What do they need to know? 'Know' covers both what they need to imagine and invent, to create characters of sufficient depth and detail, but what facts they need to research about the world in which the event took place.

- Although they need to know, it doesn't necessarily mean that they need to show the audience. Therefore, what do they need to show? And, equally important, what do they *not* need to show? Is it a gap that will leave the audience floundering?

The group should also be aware that all decisions regarding content and sequence are provisional and may alter in the final stage! Depending on the event you choose, and the focus and theme that emerges, an understanding of the forms and conventions of agitprop and political theatre (particularly Brechtian) is useful. However, as mentioned in the answer to Question 11 in Part 1, steer the group away from hectoring the audience: they are not individually or collectively responsible for the injustice depicted.

It is useful to impose some overall criteria. Some suggestions:

- The piece should switch perspective on events at some point during the action.

- The piece should include a slow-motion sequence as a key moment in the narrative.
- No dialogue in the first scene. This involves revisiting the opening scene created in Activity 1 – but then, that should be revisited anyway. As the work develops, it may not be the most effective place to start.

Finally, if the event chosen involves violence or death, it may be appropriate to specify that we do not see the deaths, although we may hear the voices of those that died. Or, if we do see, for instance, the Guildford pub bombing, there should be no physical contact, no naturalistic dialogue and that the event should be stylised in some way. For me, this is a matter of both taste and of honouring the memories of real people. I wonder, as I am sure you have done, what the relatives of those who died think of the various films about the destruction of the World Trade Center or the recent film, *The Impossible*, in which the 2004 tsunami becomes a picturesque backdrop for a heart-warming story starring Ewan McGregor and Naomi Watts? I am not suggesting that recent events cannot or should not be depicted on stage. But I am suggesting that real people and real events should be treated with respect and with dignity.

3. Rehearsing

For general guidance on Stage 3 of the devising process, see pages 143–146.

Montage

This structure offers a thematic starting point that supports those students who are skilled at making connections and drawing out themes. The structure uses a montage approach, derived from the process or technique of selecting, editing and piecing together separate sections of film to form a continuous whole. For 'sections of film', substitute: a series of scenes, images, moments on a given theme, rather than a linear narrative. Montage is an appropriate form for those who find structuring long-form, linear narratives tricky but who are comfortable working in more abstract ways and taking risks.

In a montage piece, the meaning emerges through the juxtaposition and combination of scenes. There is no obligation for the performers to join the dots, provide the answers or tie up loose ends: the audience creates their own resonance and connection. The piece will need a linking device but this will enable your students to demonstrate their understanding of use of form. Indeed, this approach galvanises understanding of the connection between form and content. For what is the fragmentation involved in montage other than use of form?

I've used surveillance and suspicion as the theme, because both are accessible to the teenage imagination and experience. However, the montage approach can be applied to any theme. What interests them? And you? And why? Of course, if your exam board assigns a theme, you could use that.

Whatever theme you apply, you need a range of stimulus material, as the following structure suggests. It may be that any one of the stimulus and activities generate enough interest and possibilities to provide the basis for an entire piece.

1. Generating and Exploring

1. Ask the group to create a spidergram based on the word: *suspicion*. They should use this spidergram to create an abstract piece that communicates the atmosphere and mood they associate with that word. No words allowed but sounds are acceptable.

If your group is not used to working in non-naturalistic ways, ask each individual to create a series of six movements, which are then repeated, with an accompanying sound. The juxtaposition of the individual activities within the group creates images and meaning for the audience to interpret. If necessary, suggest a sequence of movements.

Show the piece to another group or to the whole class. The audience response will inform the group's subsequent planning and the development of their ideas. To maximise the usefulness of this, ensure that the audience know before they see the work that:

- Everyone in the audience must respond with an image, a story, a feeling triggered by what they have seen.
- Everyone in the audience must express their views positively.

It goes without saying that a member of the group should record all the responses, to inform future work.

2. Practically anything by Franz Kafka plunges us into a world of suspicion and paranoia. Equally important, as you know if you have used any dramatisation of his short story, *Metamorphosis*, he is particularly amenable to expressionistic interpretations, where the world is presented from the subjective perspective of the protagonist.

This activity uses the opening of Kafka's novel *The Trial* (written in 1914 or '15 but not published until 1925, a year after the author's death). Ask the group to dramatise the extract. They should use the dialogue contained in the extract and as much of the rest of the text as they think is required to tell the story. They should decide whether the best way of doing this is to have a separate narrator or whether to have actors moving from speaking to the audience in the third person to speaking to each other in the first person (see also Exercise 41 on moving from first to third person in Part 3 of this book). They should use their knowledge of gesture, tone, silence and speech to create an atmosphere of tension and the sense of a world in which such events can take place. It is also important that they do not try to 'solve' the story: the whole point is that the nature of K's crime, if he has committed one, remains unknown to him and to the audience.

The Trial
by Franz Kafka
translated by David Wyllie

Someone must have been telling lies about Josef K. He knew he had done nothing wrong but, one morning, he was arrested. Every day at eight in the morning he was brought his breakfast by Mrs Grubach's cook – Mrs Grubach was his landlady – but today she didn't come. That had never happened before.

K. waited a little while, looked from his pillow at the old woman who lived opposite and who was watching him with an inquisitiveness quite unusual for her, and finally, both hungry and disconcerted, rang the bell. There was immediately a knock at the door and a man entered. He had never seen the man in this house before. He was slim but firmly built, his clothes were black and close-fitting, with many folds and pockets, buckles and buttons and a belt, all of which gave the impression of being very practical but without making it very clear what they were actually for.

'Who are you?' asked K., sitting half upright in his bed. The man, however, ignored the question as if his arrival simply had to be accepted, and merely replied, 'You rang?' 'Anna should have brought me my breakfast,' said K. He tried to work out who the man actually was, first in silence, just through observation and by thinking about it, but the man didn't stay still to be looked at for very long. Instead he went over to the door, opened it slightly, and said to someone who was clearly standing immediately behind it, 'He wants Anna to bring him his breakfast.'

There was a little laughter in the neighbouring room, it was not clear from the sound of it whether there were several people laughing. The strange man could not have learned anything from it that he hadn't known already, but now he said to K., as if making his report 'It is not possible.'

'It would be the first time that's happened,' said K., as he jumped out of bed and quickly pulled on his trousers. 'I want to see who that is in the next room, and why it is that Mrs Grubach has let me be disturbed in this way.' It immediately occurred to him that he needn't have said this out loud, and that he must to some extent have acknowledged their authority by doing so, but that didn't seem important to him at the time. That, at least, is how the stranger took it, as he said, 'Don't you think you'd better stay where you are?'

'I want neither to stay here nor to be spoken to by you until you've introduced yourself.'

'I meant it for your own good,' said the stranger and opened the door, this time without being asked.

3. Ask the group to research surveillance and/or present them with the following facts:

- Britain has more than four million closed-circuit security cameras, more than any other Western democracy.
- One-fifth of the world's CCTV cameras are in Britain.
- The average Briton is captured on as many as three hundred cameras every day, usually unaware that their movements are observed and recorded.
- Increasingly, our mobile phones and our computers can be used to provide information about what we do and where we do it.

Ask the group to create a series of five vignettes, featuring a protagonist who is observed and whose paranoia increases with every observation.

No vignette should last longer than one minute. Each one should begin and/or finish with the same frozen image. At some point in the sequence, whatever or whoever is observing the protagonist should start communicating with him or her, commenting on his or her behaviour.

4. The personification of death occurs in numerous stories, songs, films and images. Ask the students in the group to find visual images of death personified. Or, if you doubt their research abilities, provide them with an appropriate image of the Grim Reaper. (The lyrics to the Appalachian folk ballad, 'O Death', from the movie *O Brother, Where Art Thou?* are also useful). Ask them to create a scene where someone encounters their own death personified. Or perhaps, given the overall theme, attempts to avoid encountering their own death personified.

5. Ask your students to find out what a dystopian community or society means. They may well know already: dystopian fiction is big amongst teenagers who read: *The Hunger Games* novels by Suzanne Collins and Charlie Higson's 'all adults are zombies' series *The Enemy* spring to mind. Any film set in a post-apocalyptic landscape is more likely to be dystopian than utopian too.

If your students have read *1984* in English (and the chances are that they have), you could refer them to that, in particular the phrase 'Big Brother is Watching You'. Ask them to create a scene that shows a dystopian world from the point of view of the characters who control it – with particular emphasis on their attitude to those who are controlled? Other useful reference points to research are the notion of the panopticon (as invented by Jeremy Bentham), or images of control and suppression, such as Gustav Doré's illustration *Newgate Exercise Yard*. Whatever form the piece takes, it should feature repeated movement or gesture.

2. Selecting, Structuring and Developing

The group now has a series of variations on the central theme, using a range of forms and conventions which can be explored, developed and used (or not) in their final piece.

The following points should be made and considered:

- How does each of these episodes, whether mini-narratives or mood pieces, elucidate their theme?
- What would be the effect if each began or finished with the same image, or line?
- What will be the linking device to move from one episode to the next?

Montage is a way of using form which occurs in the work of such playwrights as Caryl Churchill. Both *Soft Cops* (1984) and *Love and Information* (2012) are worth assigning as background research for the group: there may even be scenes that can be incorporated into their own montage piece. Or Bertolt Brecht's *Fear and Misery of the Third Reich* (1938), which creates a series of vignettes that, taken together, present a picture of the world described in the title.

Given, too, that montage is amenable to the use of expressionistic conventions, it is particularly important that students consider such aspects of expressionism as:

- The heightened, stylised, non-naturalistic nature of the genre.
- The focus on the internal world of the protagonist exposed to the audience, and the possibility of the audience feeling and experiencing what the protagonist is experiencing.
- Different people playing different aspects of the same character.
- Theatre as an assault on the senses.

The group will have their own experiences of suspicion, whether feeling suspicious or being the subject of suspicion, and surveillance. To develop further sequences for possible inclusion, use the format outlined in Exercise 12 (page 172) in Part 3.

As the group revisit and develop the work generated in Stage 1, suggest they do so in the following ways:

- Find a piece of music that enhances the atmosphere of the abstract piece created for Activity 1. The music could be used as part of the linking device/motif. Or perhaps Activity 1 itself could be the linking device?

- Activity 2 mentions expressionistic techniques. The technique of putting the audience in the position of the protagonist might be considered for this, or for another sequence.

- Develop Activity 5 to include consideration of the advantages of surveillance and ways in which they benefit society, even if they may constrain individual freedom.

It is very important that, throughout this stage and into the final stage, the group continue to experiment with the overall sequence of episodes: as suggested in the introduction, different juxtapositions will create different meanings and resonances for the audience.

3. Rehearsing

For general guidance on Stage 3 of the devising process, see pages 143–146.

We All Come From Somewhere Else

This structure allows students to use their family histories and their own experiences as the basis for their work. This creates a degree of ownership of the material that supports high attainment. It also provides a high level of emotional engagement with the characters they portray. There are plenty of antecedents for family history and personal experience as the basis for devised theatre. The original *We All Come From Somewhere Else* was an extra-curricular theatre project that I made with students from three secondary schools in the London Borough of Newham in 1995. Students interviewed their families and their testimony was used as the basis for some scenes and monologues, interspersed with scenes dramatising historical events in Newham. The project was inspired by the *Motherland* project, co-coordinated by Elyse Dodgson and Marcia Smith at the turn of the 1980s, where African-Caribbean girls created work based on their mothers' experiences of coming to Britain in the 1950s. (The book, *Motherland*, which resulted from the project, is long out of print but second-hand copies are still available online.)

The representation of family experiences celebrates and affirms the background of the performers, without trapping them in their immediate experience. While most of my teaching experience has been in culturally diverse schools, yours does not need to be. For truly, we *all* come from somewhere else. Some of us have moved from one country to another, or one part of the country to another. Because we wanted to or because we had to. People who have always lived in the same place come from somewhere else too because, as someone once said, 'The past is another country.' Or, as Barack Obama said, in his first presidential inauguration speech, 'Let us mark this day with remembrance of who we are and how far we have travelled.' The key theme is the relationship between the past and the present.

In the specific is the universal, regardless of the ethnicity or diversity of your students. One of the potential benefits of this structure is that it enables both performers and audience to discover what unites rather than divides them. However, it should be noted that it requires students who are not only committed to the necessary research and preparation, but are also open to sharing their family histories and experiences.

1. Generating and Exploring

1. Seeing from a different perspective is fundamental to the activities in this structure. So this activity is a good starting point because it involves:

- Describing from a different point of view leading to empathy with that point of view.
- Precision and selectivity in speech/description.
- Challenging what we assume regarding shared experience, understanding and knowledge when we communicate.

It is also useful more generally if a student is playing a character from a different place and time, so can be used in that context too.

The premise is that the student is a caveman or woman transported to the present day who is trying to describe something of which they have no understanding. Perhaps a telephone, a cash machine, a television (are those very small people imprisoned in there?) or a letterbox (are those people feeding it?). Individually and simultaneously, within the group, each student creates a solo spontaneous improvisation, exploring the imaginary object, establishing their character's reaction to it, whether bewilderment, fear, wonder or a combination of the three.

Next, in turn, each member describes what they have seen, without naming the object, and using appropriate childlike, naive and simple language. They should incorporate their feelings about it and what function they think it has, in this strange new world in which they find themselves. As soon as a listener thinks they know what is being described, they should put their hand up. If their identification is correct, move on to the next description.

To prepare for subsequent work, ask the group to conclude with a discussion on what objects that we take for granted would be viewed with the same lack of comprehension by people who lived fifty years ago? And which by people who lived one hundred years ago?

2. The next stage requires photographs of people from bygone days. You could provide these, although it is better if the students bring in family photos of their ancestors.

Regardless of which of the above you choose, ask the group to sit in a circle, with the various photos displayed within the circle. Around the circle, ask each student to state where in this country or another country they were born, and whether at home or hospital. Then where their mother was born, then their father. Then grandparents. Then – if they can – their great-grandparents. Make it clear that there are various acceptable and understandable reasons why a person might not know. Their findings should, of course, be recorded – perhaps on a map of the world or the country, depending on how far-flung the places of birth are.

Next comes a solo spontaneous activity. Each person imagines that there is an old-fashioned outfit or different style of clothing on a chair. What they picture should be based on the picture of an ancestor provided, given that older pictures are likely to be a formally posed portrait. The purpose of the activity is to mime putting that outfit on: what's the texture, weight, how does it affect movement?

Ask the group to develop the solo spontaneous work into a mime or movement piece showing a typical moment in the typical day of the person they are depicting. Of course, the person might not be wearing the outfit in the picture: photographs were a luxury and tended to feature people dressed in their Sunday best.

These individual mimes should be combined into a group piece, simply by performing them at the same time. However, the group should consider how they put the individual sequences together. Should they start and end simultaneously or are the sequences staggered? Do some people freeze or pause while others continue? No words are allowed but they could add music.

The activity will lead them to an awareness of gaps in their knowledge. This could be consolidated by hot-seating. Each person becomes their ancestor, while the rest of the group pose questions. Each character is allowed to say, 'I don't know, I need to find out.' This will indicate what research is required, should any of these characters be developed in Stage 2.

3. For the next activity, each participant needs to identify and interview an older relative. I assigned the following questions:

- When did you come to [wherever you live now] and why?
- What were your first impressions when you arrived?
- How did your parents meet?
- What's the most frightening experience you've ever had?
- What was the happiest day of your life, so far?
- What was the saddest day of your life, so far?
- What were your school days like?
- Were your parents strict?
- What is the biggest change you have seen since your childhood?
- Who lived in your house before you?
- How did you meet your partner?

I also asked students to decide on three additional questions. These might be supplementary to a question above, or might venture into a different area of experience. Ideally, the responses will be recorded (and many students will have smartphones which enable them to do so), thus enabling the possibility of using actual voices in the final piece.

Once the interviews have been conducted, the group should share their findings. Next, they should agree on a story that has emerged from the interviews to dramatise. The piece should have a narrator. This is the older relative. However, the group should decide whether that character speaks directly to the audience or whether the interviewer is represented on stage. The group should also decide whether the same actor plays the older and younger versions of the character. If so, how do they move between the past and the present? If played by two different actors, how do they make the connection clear?

Stress that they should not adapt or augment the story. The point is not to make it more 'interesting' or 'dramatic', but to honour it.

4. Within the group, and using information collected in their research interviews and discussed at the end of Activity 1, discuss what do students think are the biggest technological or social changes that have occurred in their lifetimes? This may also involve the key differences between 'then and there' – whenever and wherever the ancestor lived – and 'here and now'. If you think that some of the group are inclined to be passengers, ask them to work individually to create their own lists, or subdivide the group into pairs and smaller groups.

You might wish to narrow the scope of the activity, by specifying an area of focus, such as home, school, work, methods of transport or communication. You may also wish to provide pictures of then and now to scaffold the task for students.

Next, the group should create a two-minute scene dramatising the difference. The group should assign one person to act as director, providing an outside eye. Ask them to focus on which theatrical convention or conventions will best enable them to communicate, theatrically, the difference. However, outlaw the use of a narrator: they've used that convention in the previous exercise. When showing, bear in mind my earlier comments on the need to accurately create and represent the world. So, if necessary, discuss and modify historically inaccurate language, behaviour or artefacts.

5. In pairs, within the group, brainstorm reasons why people – as individuals or as communities – might move or migrate. They should include any reasons that have come up in their interviews or that they

know from their various family histories. If they need some suggestions to get them going, try:

- Education
- Love
- Family
- War
- Natural disasters
- Poverty/opportunity

Now ask the group to find testimony about the experience of arriving in a new place, as well as photographs. Again, some of these may come from their interviews with family members. Others can be found by accessing any oral-history archive online, or books about the experience of change and migration. Ideally, they will find at least half a dozen short quotes about the experience. If you doubt their ability to remember to research, have the student resource sheet on the following page available.

The group should create a piece on arrival, inspired by and using the images and personal testimony quotes provided on the experience of arriving in a new and strange place. When I used this exercise, I stipulated repetition (of words, movement or gesture): impose whichever criteria you think will galvanise use of the medium and elements of theatre to create a non-naturalistic piece.

You might think that scenes about arriving in a new place should begin a process. In fact, their placement here is strategic. This is partly because the previous work creates a knowledge base which will lead to scenes of greater understanding and therefore of meaning. It is also because, by concluding this stage of the devising process, it opens up a potential focus for all the material collected so far.

Arrival: Personal Testimony

I expected something beautiful but at the time it was very very dirty and everything seemed to be so black. We were very distressed. We arrived about half-past eleven in the evening. It was raining – awful, terrible weather it was.

I was very homesick. It looked very different. It was a big city and I come from a very small island. I was a bit confused. The first time I went on the Underground I got lost.

My friend came to meet me at Waterloo. The scene was just a lot of people. Everybody who come off the train and who come to meet relatives. So it was just a big crowd of people.

There was curious onlookers standing around looking: anxious black people and curious white people.

I was on the train and when I looked out through the window and see all these little houses and outside is so black, I said to somebody, 'When are we going to reach England?'

My husband came to meet me, everything was strange.

Nowhere to live, nowhere to sleep, nowhere – nobody wanted to know you. If I had money I would have gone back straight away.

When you arrive, people try to communicate with you through sign language or they shout at you. They think perhaps by shouting they can make you understand what they are talking about.

It was a feeling of total confusion having to go through immigration and all the people around you that you didn't know. I felt utterly despairing. It was a feeling of total confusion because I suddenly realised I'd arrived, I'd left home and I arrived here.

I cried like a baby the first week I was here. You had to be at work by 6.30 a.m. If you were late you would be disciplined.

> At the time you used to get signs saying, 'No Irish, no Blacks'. You know, that saddened me, coming from a place where they tell you this is the mother country.
>
> You had to keep your dignity. A lot of boys came here and had mental breakdowns because of that stress.

2. Selecting, Structuring and Developing

You have *change* (whether personal or historical, as in the difference between then and now) as a potential starting point. You have *arrival in a new place* as a potential starting point. You have a range of family stories from which to select. You are spoilt for choice!

In this structure, students have a great deal of information to work with regarding the characters they portray. Nevertheless, they should still refer to student resource sheets 1 and 3. Exercises regarding characterisation from Part 3: Refining, Troubleshooting and Finishing can also be assigned as part of this stage of the devising process, as required.

Student resource sheets 2 and 4 will support how they construct individual scenes and sequences. However, the overarching question is whether to weave together multiple narratives or whether to focus on a single story. If the group decide on the former, the question is:

- What is the common theme and how will the scenes be linked?

If the group decide on the latter, the question to ask is:

- Will the story sustain an entire piece? It may do, but they may also wish to consider using the same narrative but from different perspectives.

As with other structures, it is useful to refer the group to various plays. *Motherland* (2008) by Steve Gilroy (and no relation to the *Motherland* project mentioned in the introduction to *We All Come From Somewhere*

Else) uses testimony and true stories of women affected by recent conflicts in Iraq and Afghanistan. *Kindertransport* (1993) by Diane Samuels is fictional but its narrative structure moves backwards and forwards in time, in order to communicate the effect of the past on the present. *The Pride* (2008) by Alexi Kaye Campbell moves backwards and forwards between two gay men and a woman, who exist in 1958 and in the present; their relationships and choices have differed because of the different social codes of each era. In Scene 9 of *Fen* (Caryl Churchill, again, in 1983), the ghost of a rural worker coexists with two contemporary characters, and rails against both what has changed and what remains the same. It's another useful device for communicating the relationship between past and present. However, ensure the group bear in mind that the contrast between then and now is not, in and of itself, enough: there has to be some reason to compare and contrast, and a reason and focus for such a narrative.

Various linking devices and conventions have already been suggested in Stage 1 of this structure. Here are some other possibilities to suggest:

- The divided self: two actors play the same character at different stages – the older version interrogating the younger version.
- Using an object, perhaps the story of a suitcase, as the framing device.
- Flashback structure where an old person looks back on his or her life.
- Repetition of a key line of text or gesture or action which comes to symbolise the experience of change or arrival or whatever they identify as their main theme.
- Location as a unifying device. It could be a specific room or place where all the events depicted have taken place. It could be what has occurred in the same house over several generations. Or – here's one that I have borrowed in the past – in *The Brother from Another Planet* (the 1984 film by John Sayles): an alien crash-lands at the former Ellis Island immigration centre. When he touches the walls, he can hear the voices of those who have been 'processed' there. This can be adapted and used as a way of animating, freezing and moving between narratives.

The same principles regarding use of testimony and allowing real characters their dignity that are discussed in Stage 2 of the Reportage structure apply here too.

The group should also be aware that all decisions regarding content and sequence are provisional and may alter in the final stage!

3. Rehearsing

For general guidance on Stage 3 of the devising process, see pages 143–146.

No Inspiration Required

This structure is particularly appropriate for kinaesthetic learners, as well as those who lack the confidence to be inspired and for those inclined to sit, endlessly, when they should be on their feet, working. Movement sequences can be an excellent starting point for theatre: kinaesthetic working not only bypasses conscious decisions, but avoids the pitfalls of working out the plot in advance, too! It also reinforces the importance of doing rather than describing or discussing.

The activities, which can be done in any sequence, offer a series of actions and/or a line or two of dialogue while – deliberately – avoiding providing a context for them. Possible locations, characters, circum-stances emerge in two ways:

- Quite literally going through the motions generates ideas and possibilities for the performers.
- Showing the work to another group – or the whole class – creates other possible meanings, interpretations and directions.

When showing work, as with the first activity in Structure 3: Montage, it is important that:

- Everyone in the audience responds with an image, a story, a feeling which is triggered by what they have seen.
- Everyone in the audience expresses their views positively.
- A member of the group records all the responses to inform future work.

In each of the activities outlined in Stage 1, ask the students to enact the actions described. If sufficient possibilities emerge from the first activity, or the second, you may not need to go through all the subse-quent ones.

As with other structures, not all the members of the group need to participate in each activity. Where there are more in the group than are required for the activity, the remainder can direct, observe and shape, as well as suggest possible meanings and contexts.

1. Generating and Exploring

All the following activities require a hard copy of the sequence of movement, as the idea at this stage is to replicate rather than necessarily remember the sequence. All scenes that result should be shown, in order to raise possibilities.

1. For a pair. Or for two or more sets of pairs, given that the outcome will be different.

A is a person packing up a room (this is mimed, of course). No dialogue. B is another character who is watching. The pair need to experiment to decide:

- Whether B is present from the start.
- Whether B is standing or sitting.
- Whether A acknowledges B's presence in any way during the scene.

When A is finished, they pause for five seconds precisely. B says to A: 'It's time to go now.'

A does not respond.

You can stipulate the length the scene should be. Thirty seconds should suffice.

2. For four people, who should decide who is A, who B, who C and who D.

Prepare the following sequence of movements. No dialogue should be added.

- There are three chairs.
- A is walking up and down.
- B enters and sits on one chair. They tap their foot, repeatedly.
- C enters. A keeps walking up and down, B keeps tapping.
- C exits.
- D enters.
- B stands.
- D takes B's seat.
- A pauses. Then continues walking up and down.
- B exits.
- C enters again. Sits on another chair.
- D and C make eye contact.
- A stops walking. Opens their mouth, as if about to speak. The scene ends at this point.

What they might say is part of the feedback. Also ask those in the scene who they think they are, where they are, what the relationships between characters might be, particularly their relative status.

3. Assign one or use both of the following solo sequences, which should be improvised spontaneously.

a) There is an empty chair in an empty room. A person walks in and sits on the chair. The rest of the group watch, then suggest:

- Who is the person? For instance: old, young, high or low status?
- Where is the person? Is it a familiar place or a strange place?
- What has just happened?
- What is about to happen?
- What is the person feeling? How can we tell?

The same performer repeats the sequence, taking on as many of the suggestions received as are compatible with each other. In addition, they should also add miming stepping through the door to the room: is it easy to open? Do they have a key? And so on . . .

Different members of the group can repeat the same sequence, with the other members of the group watching and interpreting, as above.

As well or instead, try the following, longer sequence. It is adapted – well, stolen – from the opening of *The Web*, an early (1913) one-act play by Eugene O'Neill. Any play which specifies a sequence of actions can be used to create a similar exercise.

b) The character mimes the following in the specified order. They may refer to the list of instructions as they do so: the purpose is not to test their memory but to see what the sequence suggests, both to the performer and to those watching. For this reason, it is useful to have someone who can read the sequence out so that, the first time through, the performer does not know what comes next.

The character:

- Sits (and remains so until the ninth action in the sequence).
- Smokes.
- Glance over to a bed.
- Coughs.
- Lifts handkerchief to mouth.
- Looks at handkerchief.
- Throws cigarette on table.
- Coughs.
- Stands.
- Goes to bed (to look at whoever is there, not to sleep).
- Bends.
- Kisses whoever is in bed.
- Goes to mirror.

The sequence should be performed twice: neutrally the first time then, the second time through, with whatever mood or emotion seems appropriate to the performer.

The audience should respond to what they see using the same questions as for Activity 3a.

4. Dialogue can come before character and location. Indeed, Sarah Kane, Simon Stephens and Martin Crimp have all written plays where the script does not assign speeches to specific characters. Use the following brief dialogue, or create your own, for a pair to enact. While they may make decisions about who the characters are, where they are and to what they refer, the scene should nevertheless be shown to others, to facilitate further options and choices.

A. Well?

B *does not respond.*

A. Well?

B *does not respond.*

A. Did you go there?

There is a pause. B nods.

B. I found this note. (*Reads the following.*) 'I am what I am. I see the nature of my offence. It is finished. It is finished.'

5. Another pair activity (although two different pairs can work simultaneously and create two different versions).

The pair sits opposite each other. They have a muttered conversation. They can talk gibberish, if they wish: the point is that the audience do not know what they are saying and, at this point, the actors do not need to know what or who is being discussed.

Stipulate that there will be three pauses. The pair should work out when. During each pause, each person should look left or look right or look up or look down. They could both do the same but do not have to. The looks might be simultaneous but do not have to be. One might be in response to the other. The pair should not make any decisions about why the pause or why the look in whatever direction: the point, as with preceding activities, is to allow the audience to interpret what is going on and, perhaps, why.

2. Selecting, Structuring and Developing

Depending on the number in the group, you may wish to assign different activities to different pairs and individuals, then have them working simultaneously. Whatever way you organise Stage 1 of No Inspiration Required, the more people who see the work and provide suggestions as to context, location and who the characters might be, the better.

The group now has numerous possible interpretations and contexts for at least five scenes. The key questions to pose are:

• Which ones link?

• Which ones could become part of the same narrative?

I suggest that the group puts each suggestion as to what each scene might be onto a separate card and arrange the cards into different sequences that suggest different possible narratives. They should develop whichever they feel is the most powerful and engaging, both to the group and for the audience.

Whichever narrative they develop is likely to be character-driven. Student resource sheets 1 and 3 (pages 147 and 149) will provide general guidance regarding how to create characters with sufficient depth and detail. Exercises regarding characterisation from Part 3: Refining, Troubleshooting and Finishing can also be assigned as part of this stage of the devising process, as required.

Whatever narrative emerges, there are likely to be gaps. While they need to fill in these gaps, it doesn't necessarily mean that they need to show the audience. Therefore, they should consider what do they need to show. And, equally important, what do they *not* need to show? Is it a gap that will leave the audience floundering? If it does, does it matter? The nature of this structure might lead to an unresolved ending, overall or in certain scenes.

It may be that several possible narratives emerge; in which case, it is worth referring to this stage of Structure 7: The Multiple Protagonist for further ideas about how to structure the material.

3. Rehearsing

For general guidance on Stage 3 of the devising process, see pages 143–146.

This Woman's Work

This structure uses three-dimensional conceptual art as an inspiration and a springboard. It does not adapt so much as transmute. It is not a suitable starting point for all students, not least because many people find the whole notion of conceptual art baffling and irritating. It is, though, the type of stimulus that can lead to great work from students who can deal with an open-ended, thematic approach which requires both the ability to work in abstract and symbolic ways, and who have the ability, individually and collectively, to make imaginative leaps.

It is notable that many of the great conceptual artists in the last half-century have been women. I'm thinking of such artists as Cornelia Parker, Louise Bourgeois, Rachel Whiteread, Tracey Emin. In Emin and Bourgeois's work, their experience of being female is central to their art. Both Parker and Whiteread are less immediately concerned with their personal experience. Cornelia Parker has said: 'I resurrect things that have been killed off . . . My work is all about the potential of materials – even when it looks like they've lost all possibilities.' Whiteread's works are casts of what is best described as negative space, whether an entire house, a water tower or a collection of the spaces under an assortment of chairs and stools. She says the casts carry 'the residue of years and years of use'. I would say that she makes the invisible visible and tangible, and makes the absent present: little wonder then, that she was commissioned to make the Vienna Holocaust memorial (aka *Nameless Library*), unveiled in 2000.

I've used *Cold Dark Matter: An Exploded View* (1991), as the stimulus for this structure. For this installation, Cornelia Parker arranged for the British Army to blow up a garden shed. She then suspended the fragments and shards of wood as if capturing and freezing the very moment of the explosion. In the centre was a light that cast the shadows of the wood on the walls of the room where it was installed. However, *House* (and other sculptures) by Rachel Whiteread, *My Bed* by Tracey Emin and practically anything by Louise Bourgeois could be substituted. Also, although she's a visual artist, rather than a conceptual one, Frida Kahlo's self-portraits, in particular *Cracked Spine*, are also relevant. All can be readily found in any image search.

Sol LeWitt, the American (male) conceptual artist, who died in 2007, wrote that:

> In conceptual art the idea or concept is the most important
> aspect of the work. When an artist uses a conceptual form
> of art, it means that all of the planning and decisions are
> made beforehand and the execution is a perfunctory affair.
> The idea becomes a machine that makes the art.

We may quibble with the word 'perfunctory', but what I like about this quote is the attention it draws to the parallels between conceptual art and the devising process. In both processes, the importance of the starting point is crucial, as is the planning and the decisions involved in the making, and the implicit connection between theme (or concept) and form.

By the way, despite the title of this unit, I do not suggest that it should be confined to girls' groups!

1. Generating and Exploring

1. Display the picture of *Cold Dark Matter: An Exploded View*. Do not explain its origins yet. Instead, ask the group to brainstorm their responses to the work. Make it clear that they should all accept everyone else's responses and that they should not censor their imaginations.

Cold Dark Matter: An Exploded View by Cornelia Parker

Next, explain the origins of the piece and the manner of its creation. What does the information about the methodology that created the piece add to their responses? This second wave of responses should be recorded in a different colour to the first.

Ask everyone in the group to assign a response from the first set of responses to another person in the group. Ask everyone in the group to assign a response from the second set of responses to another person in the group.

Each person in the group should create a solo still image that embodies the first response and another one for the second. They should also decide, individually, how they will transform from the first to the second. Particular attention should be paid to the rhythm and tempo of that transition: do they dissolve from one to another or is it a series of sharp, jerky movements?

The piece should be shown – or perhaps exhibited is a more apt word – in the following way. Ask the audience to sit in a large circle: the four or five members of the group should create their starting image in the middle of the circle, far enough from each other to allow those watching to walk amongst the newly created statues. The group should also be given a minute or so to decide what will trigger the transformation from one image to the next: is it when someone passes them? When the viewer pauses to look at them? Or perhaps when eye contact is made?

Ask someone from the audience to walk amongst and between the statues. Send in a couple of others. It may be that you wait until the first person has finished, or the visitors could overlap.

Get feedback from the audience on what the exhibition seemed to represent, or what mood or atmosphere it created. Make sure that you ask for the responses not only from those who had moved through, but also from those who watched them moving through.

2. Ask everyone in the group to write a short story, poem or monologue, inspired by *Cold Dark Matter*. To maximise time for practical work, I suggest that this task is set as homework, in preparation for your next session.

Each participant tells their story (or reads it) to the group. Don't suggest that they will be dramatised, although they may be as part of Stage 2 of the devising process.

3. Give the group the caption, 'The Machine that Makes the Art', taken from the Sol LeWitt quote, above. Their task is to collectively create that machine.

They should create a group still image as the starting point, then animate it. Ask each member of the group to step out of the piece as they work to adjust and reorganise the movement as required, to heighten the sense of a machine creating the art. The group should also play with rhythm and tempo – including slow motion, fast forward and rewind – to make it more mechanical. They may add sounds and up to three words, which may be repeated as often as they see fit, in whatever tones they think work best.

4. Give each member of the group a piece of fabric and a neutral mask. Each piece should be at least a metre wide and at least four metres long. (To source such lengths of fabric cheaply, try a trip to the local market or sari shop. The expenditure is worth it. The fabric will always come in handy for other projects.)

Assign the criterion that the piece must begin with unison movement, perhaps folding or unfolding the pieces of fabric. The piece should express the tensions and pressures that the group feel typify the life of a young woman here and now. The fabric should be used throughout.

5. Ask the group to consider why would someone create *Cold Dark Matter* (or whichever piece you are using as your starting point). You may wish to give them the earlier quotation from Cornelia Parker about the artist's perception of the nature of her work. However, their focus should be what they think the artist might want to express about the world, herself or her experience (in general or in response to a particular event).

The group should then create a monologue which might be spoken by the artist. However, they should find a way of dividing the speech up between the members of the group. As a criterion, specify that it should include two repeated phrases, one of which should be the title of the artwork.

Show the piece to another group or to the whole class. The audience response will inform the group's subsequent planning and the development of their ideas. To maximise the usefulness of this, ensure that the audience know before they see the work that:

- Everyone in the audience must respond with an image, a story, a feeling which is triggered by what they have seen.
- Everyone in the audience must express their views positively.

2. Selecting, Structuring and Developing

This is perhaps the hardest structure to suggest what should happen in Stage 2, simply because of the range of possibilities and directions that have been generated by Stage 1.

- If the group are foregrounding the (female) artist's experience and her means of self-expression, does it become a piece about the artist herself? If this is the case, you should ensure that they research the artist and her other work.
- Do the group take one of the stories, poems or monologues they have written in Activity 2 as the basis for their work?
- Given that both Activities 1 and 5 involve soliciting responses from the whole class, is the group's piece a response to one or more of those responses?

Although it is likely that characters (in the naturalistic sense) are less important in this structure than others, they still need to be aware of the need to characterise. Student resource sheets 1 and 3 (pages 147 and 149) will support this.

If the form that emerges has an episodic structure, the group need to consider:

- How does each of these episodes, whether mini-narratives or mood pieces, elucidate their theme?
- What would be the effect if each began or finished with the same image, or line?
- What will be the linking device to move from one episode to the next? Perhaps the 'machine' that emerged from Activity 3 could be used?

Given, too, that conceptual art is amenable to the use of expressionistic conventions, it is particularly important that students consider such aspects of expressionism as:

- The heightened, stylised, non-naturalistic nature of the genre.
- The focus on the internal world of the protagonist exposed to the audience, and the possibility of the audience feeling and experiencing what the protagonist is experiencing.
- Different people playing different aspects of the same character.
- Theatre as an assault on the senses.

If the group are taken with developing Activity 4 and the use of fabric in their piece, they should search for images of *Lamentation*, a solo, seated dance choreographed and first performed by Martha Graham in the early 1930s, where the dancer is wrapped and sometimes shrouded in fabric. They may also wish to research the theatre practitioner Meyerhold and his symbolist style of theatrical representation.

3. Rehearsing

For general guidance on Stage 3 of the devising process, see pages 143–146.

The Multiple Protagonist

This structure, where each actor leads a scene, and where a framing or linking device connects them all in some way, has many advantages. It does not require the group to be skilled at constructing a long-form narrative. The framework is a given, as is the ensemble nature of the piece. It can be useful for a group with an erratic attender: their story can be removed, if required, so long as the roles they play in other scenes are kept to a minimum. Because every student plays several roles, they have several opportunities to show their range.

However, there are disadvantages too. Playing multiple roles may merely highlight a candidate's lack of versatility. The plays that emerge can be over-schematic. It can be hard to avoid cliché. Every examiner will have seen rather too many pieces that begin with a therapy group, usually in treatment for alcohol or drug issues, before flashing back to four or five versions of pretty much the same story, most of them involving too much sobbing and gnashing of teeth. Sometimes, we first encounter the characters on a Tube on what turns out to be 7th July 2005. Or on their way to work at the World Trade Center on 11th September 2001. There is something slightly offensive about taking huge tragedies, removing the political context (or not displaying any understanding of that) and reducing it as a framing device for a series of miniature soap operas.

In my experience, the way to avoid this pitfall is simple: don't begin with the linking device. How and why the characters come to find themselves in the same place at the same time (if, indeed, they do) can be determined later. So this structure first creates characters, not least because, if the narrative is character-driven, it will lead to work of greater depth and detail. In Stage 1, the characters are first created and then developed through a variety of scenes, each of which reveals further aspects of the character. The characters and theme are connected. I suggest using either regret and loss or desire (not in the specifically sexual sense), because pretty much everyone has experienced both. It is only in Stage 2 of the devising process that students are asked to consider and create a context and means whereby the characters' paths cross.

1. Generating and Exploring

As you know, there are many different approaches to characterisation, some of which are discussed in Part 3 of this book. You know your students, so adapt this stage accordingly, if you wish, in order to play to their strengths. If they are better at physical ways in to character, then incorporate some of those approaches, as outlined in the characterisation exercises in Part 3: Refining, Troubleshooting and Finishing. If they respond to a more psychological approach and find it easy to make the imaginative leap into another person's experience, then emphasise the Stanislavsky questions on student resource sheet 3 (page 149). Because the work in this structure is character-driven, both student resource sheets 1 (page 147) and 3 are best introduced in Stage 1 of this particular structure.

1. For this first activity, you will need to assemble a random collection of objects, two for each member of the group. These objects could be anything: it is the group's responsibility, rather than yours, to make sense of them, which they will do by creating a short monologue explaining why the two objects they have been assigned are important to a character. They do not need to know anything else about the character at this stage nor make any decisions beyond the significance of the two objects in the person's life. Nor do the two objects have to be connected to the same episode in the person's life. So, for example, if someone is assigned a pair of shoes and an old bus ticket, the shoes might be those that they wore on an important occasion and the bus ticket was one that they saved because the journey had some significance. If they are assigned an old pocket watch and a CD, it might be that the old pocket watch belonged to a beloved elderly relative, now deceased, and the CD features a song that they associate with an important event or occasion,

whether happy or sad. Perhaps it was played at their wedding. Or at the funeral of a close relative or friend. You get the general idea.

2. Ask each student in the group to create a typical twenty-four-hour cycle for their character. They do not have to incorporate the objects from Activity 1 into Activity 2 because those objects represent or symbolise important events in their respective lives. The purpose of this activity is to explore their daily life. In order to do this, they need to make some decisions about the character such as:

- Age and gender (for the purposes of this structure, it is probably best that the character is the same gender as the actor).
- Whether the character lives alone.
- Job (if the character has one).

Next, they should each decide what they are doing at each hour of the day. I have, in the past, created a sheet with two clock faces on it, one for a.m. and one for p.m., in order that the students can plan what happens at each point. Given the amount you have to do, you may prefer for them just to list what occurs at each hour, starting at midnight.

If you think it's necessary, stipulate that these are probably ordinary people leading ordinary lives, rather than spies or international playboys.

Divide the group into two: one half calls out the hours of the day in sequence every thirty seconds for the other half whose task is to enact whatever each is doing at that time. Of course, a portion of the typical twenty-four hours will be spent asleep. However, the time they go to bed and rise, and how well they sleep, and whether their sleep is regularly disturbed (by a small child, by the need to visit the toilet or whatever else might disturb them) should feature. Then reverse so that the audience become the performers and vice versa.

3. Before embarking on this next activity, assign each of the group:

- A physical characteristic.
- A secret desire or a secret regret (depending on whether you wish to focus on *desire* or *regret* as the theme).

- A character flaw or phobia.

Assign these individually and privately: the others in the group should not be aware of them at this point.

Based on what they now know about their character, assign pairs within the group. Each pair should create two short scenes, no longer than a minute each, showing two aspects of their life. In one, the protagonist has higher status than the other character. In the other, the protagonist has lower status. The other student should play both characters encountered. The characteristic, secret desire and the character flaw or phobia do not have to be crowbarred into the action, although they might affect or inform the interaction in some way.

4. As a whole group, they should create another short scene for each character. The purpose is to illustrate what's wrong with the character's life. This is not to suggest that everything is wrong and the character spends the time in abject misery. It might be an aspect of the character's life that they wish they could change. It might be more general, such as constant worry about money. What each protagonist chooses should be informed by the work in previous activities, and should take account of their secret desire or their secret regret, without making that desire or regret explicit.

5. If further character development and background is required, ask the group to hot-seat each character. Make sure that they ask, at some point, 'What is your secret desire (or regret)?' The response may not be direct. It may even be an offended denial, depending on the role and how well the student sustains it. Whatever the case, this will open up useful areas for further questioning and for character development.

2. Selecting, Structuring and Developing

Now that the group have created five different characters, the question of how their paths cross can be addressed. I write 'how their paths cross' because, although teenagers like to tie up loose ends, the linking device does not actually have to be that all the characters are literally in the same place at the same time. Perhaps they have all met the same person (if so, that person would need to feature in each protagonist's scene). Perhaps, given the thematic link of desire or loss, the group should create an image or movement sequence expressing that theme (see also Exercises 42 and 43 regarding transitions (pages 199–200) in Part 3 of this book). Such a linking device would provide a useful and perhaps necessary contrast to the essential naturalism of each protagonist's scenes. Arthur Schnitzler's play, *La Ronde* (1897), is structured as a series of duologues. In the first scene, A meets B. Next, B meets C and so on, until the circle is completed in the final scene where D or E meets A. (Admittedly, in *La Ronde*, each scene is a sexual encounter, but it's the form rather than the content that could be appropriated!) Perhaps the linking and framing device is that each protagonist's episode begins or ends in the same way: I have used what is presented as Activity 1 in Structure 5: No Inspiration Required for this in the past. On one occasion, the group used this as the beginning of each scene, then flashed back to what had happened. On another, the group created scenes, each of which finished with the action described and the final line, 'It's time to go now.'

If the group are insistent that they want the characters to all be in the same place at the same time, and if you have chosen a secret desire, then maybe each has sold their soul to achieve that desire. If they are determined to feature a therapy or support group, I suggest you refer them to the Twelve Steps programme developed by Alcoholics Anonymous and subsequently adopted by other substance-abuse and dependency self-help groups, in particular steps 8 and 9, which are:

- Make a list of all persons we had harmed, and became willing to make amends to them all.

- Make direct amends to such people wherever possible, except when to do so would injure them or others.

Then, making amends becomes the focus of each protagonist's scene.

Because, as I mentioned in the introduction, this structure brings its own framework with it, the key questions, 'What's the story (or stories, in this instance) you want to tell?' and 'How do you want to tell this story?' are less relevant than 'What effect do you want to have on the audience?' and 'How will you create that effect?'

The following points also need to be made and considered:

- How will they distill and encapsulate each character's narrative into a single scene? Not all – if any – of the scenes and monologues developed in Stage 1 will actually feature in the eventual piece, although the background work will pay off in terms of creating backstories for each protagonist.
- How will they make clear who is the protagonist in each scene?
- How will they decide what is the best sequence for the scenes?
- Given that the structure requires everyone to play a number of supporting roles, how will they ensure that each actor makes those characters as different as possible, so that they show their range and gain marks, rather than lose marks for lack of versatility?

Given these points, student resource sheets 1 and 3 (pages 147 and 149), on creating character, are even more important than in other structures, as are the exercises regarding characterisation from Part 3: Refining, Troubleshooting and Finishing, which should also be assigned as part of this stage of the devising process, as required.

3. Rehearsing

For general guidance on Stage 3 of the devising process, see pages 143–146.

Structure 8

The Third Way

There is scripted work, there is devised work and there is the third way. A combination of scripted and devised work can be highly effective. Exam boards approve of it: as one recent chief examiner's report noted, 'it was felt this approach supported students as it gave them a clear structure in relation to content style and form, defined roles and well-crafted language to build their performances on.'

The Third Way is a structure suitable for a devising process that builds on and leads on from a play explored in a previous part of the exam specification. The prior knowledge of theme and character should lead to a deeper understanding and heighten attainment. Certainly, the plot, with or without key speeches or extracts from scenes, can provide a highly structured framework and a story to enact, where a group requires that degree of structure. However, it does require a group who are used to reading and performing scripts. This presupposes a certain level of confidence and ease with their reading skills.

I've appropriated the plots of *Doctor Faustus* or *The Alchemist* in the past. (By the way, in neither case did I ask the group to read the original play and then only extracts, once they understood the plot and themes, because of the inaccessibility of the original language: I've known professional actors with a great deal of classical experience blench at first sight of Ben Jonson!) If you want to appropriate a plot, the process is simple. Summarise the whole play in a paragraph. Summarise each scene in a sentence. What are the key points in each scene? Bob's your uncle. Novels are possible too: Dickens creates great characters and social themes, although, given the length, the plot will need some judicious pruning.

As a more creative variation, the plot of a play can be told from the perspective of a minor character. After all, it's the basis of *Rosencrantz and Guildenstern Are Dead* (1966), by Tom Stoppard. As Rosencrantz (or is it Guildenstern?) remarks in that play, 'We do on stage things that are supposed to happen off. Which is a kind of integrity, if you look on every exit as being an entrance somewhere else.' I've seen a version of *Macbeth* told from the point of view of the Porter. In the first scene of *Red Noses* (1985) by Peter Barnes, the First Attendant has a single, magnificent speech (and then expires of the Black Death), railing against

> cock-pimping scribblers . . . Always writing stories where some characters are important and others just disposable stock – First Attendant, Second Peasant, Third Guard. Stories are easier when 'tisn't possible to care for everyone equal. That's how come itty-bitty people like me come to be butchered on battlefields, die in droves . . . But we first attendants are important too. We've lives.

That's the starting point for a devising process, right there.

However, the structure that is outlined here allows rather more creative freedom. It is therefore suitable for groups that can handle using an existing script as a springboard to explore the themes and conventions of the piece.

The principle – which can be applied to the play of your choice – is to take the first scene and a key moment from later in the play, which might be the introduction of a significant character, or a moment of decision or choice. This approach offers two pivot points, as it were, around which possibilities can be explored and a narrative constructed. Using the first scene reinforces understanding of what makes a good opening, regardless of where you go from there, and regardless of whether the first scene of the source material ends up as the first scene of the group's piece.

I'm using *The Threepenny Opera* (1928) by Bertolt Brecht – the music for the songs, of course, was composed by Kurt Weill. The structure does not require a knowledge of the whole play but the structure indicates where, if you are using a play that your class have studied, their background knowledge should be utilised.

1. Generating and Exploring

1. Numerous translations of *The Threepenny Opera* are available. Pick one. Ask the group to rehearse and stage the first scene – the one where Filch the beggar approaches Mr Jeremiah Peachum, up until the point where Filch exits. There are three characters in the scene, so any others in the group can shape and direct the scene. As the group work, they should note the form and conventions that the playwright has used, in this case:

* Captions (or spoken intro).
* Direct audience address.
* Satire: a comic scene with a serious purpose.
* The characters are larger than life.

When I used this as a starting point, I asked the group to chose an appropriate stage configuration for the theme and content of the piece. You may prefer not to. However, they should decide the best way to highlight and demonstrate the conventions identified above in their interpretation of the scene.

2. Having explored the first scene and the conventions the playwright uses, the next activity takes a line from that scene which encapsulates the action of the scene and is amenable to being used to find a contemporary parallel. There are two reasons for this:

* It focuses students' attention on the plot, in preparation for the consideration of the theme and the relationship between the two.
* A contemporary parallel will help students understand the connections between their own world and the world of the play and its social and historical context. In the case of *The Threepenny Opera*, this is particularly appropriate given that it is famously an adaptation of *The Beggar's Opera* by John Gay (1728).

In this case, I've used Mr Jeremiah Peachum's line: 'My business is arousing human sympathy.' You could ask the group to find a line which summarises the action, if you prefer.

Ask the group to consider whose business, nowadays, is to arouse human sympathy. If they need prompting, suggest chuggers, the day-time TV adverts that solicit donations for animal welfare or the NSPCC, or the appeals and films that are made as part of Children in Need or Comic Relief telethons.

Their task is to create a scene which elicits sympathy for the plight of the protagonist. By stipulating the effect that the scene should have on the audience, the group's attention is focused on the best way to manipulate the audience's sympathy to achieve that effect. They should refer to the techniques used by those mentioned in the previous paragraph for tips on how to do that. However – because *The Threepenny Opera*, and, indeed, *The Beggar's Opera*, both have a satirical intent, they should choose a protagonist who, in the overall scheme of things, does not require sympathy or support. A WAG down to her last dozen pairs of shoes, perhaps, or a banker whose salary has dipped to under £100,000.

The piece should be presented with utter conviction: I believe it was the French playwright Jean Giraudoux who said that: 'The secret of success is sincerity. Once you can fake that you've got it made.' The audience response will indicate the extent to which they have succeeded!

3. *The Threepenny Opera* focuses on the underworld, which is to say a community that lives outside the law on the margins of society. There are numerous plays, novels and films which explore how the underdog or the socially excluded cope with a world where poverty and injustice prevail. Or, to put it another way, the relationship and interaction between the 'haves' and the 'have-nots'. I'm thinking of Fagin's gang in *Oliver Twist*, or the Court of Miracles in Victor Hugo's *The Hunchback of Notre-Dame*, or *City of God*, the 2002 film about life in the drug gangs of the Brazilian *favelas*. Ben Jonson's plays, particularly *The Alchemist* (1610) and *Volpone* (1606), are driven by characters who have decided that, in a corrupt world, they will con, dupe and trick their way to prosperity.

In all these works, including *The Threepenny Opera*, we are asked to engage with and even approve the behaviour of characters whose actions are disapproved of by the worlds in which they live. Often –

although this does not apply to *The Threepenny Opera* – the protagonist finds a surrogate family.

So, to open up parallels with the themes and styles of the play, ask the group to devise a scene which shows a protagonist who has fallen amongst thieves and who is being inducted into the ways of the (under) world in which they find themself. The scene should indicate the benefits to the protagonist as well as the code and rules of their new 'family'.

4. Having explored the possibilities created by the opening scene of a play, we move to the exploration of a key moment, as outlined in the introduction to this structure. I've chosen the song 'Pirate Jenny', sung by the character of that name in the scene where she makes her first appearance. There are several reasons for this:

- The use of song to comment on the action and distance the audience from the action is another important convention in Brecht's approach.
- The function of the character, Pirate Jenny, is pivotal: if she did not betray Macheath, the play would stop.

You will notice that the sequence of this activity provides a context for the song (or key moment) before introducing it. This is not necessary if you have chosen a play with which the group are already familiar, as they will already understand the relevant context.

Ask the group, individually and simultaneously, to mime a menial activity. It helps to have a metronome or a piece of music with a mechanical beat, to encourage them to heighten the physicalisation of their activity. Stipulate that, at one point in the mime, the student should freeze, turn their head toward the audience (or to an imagined viewer on stage) and stare for a count of four, then resume the mimed menial activity. At another point in the action, the student should freeze again; turn their head again, but this time smile. Again, the menial activity should resume after a count of four.

Divide the group into pairs or a pair and a trio. They should create a short scene, choosing one of the menial activities. The other actor (or actors if a trio) becomes someone of higher status. The scene should begin with a still image that uses their understanding of levels to demonstrate the relative status of the characters. The scene that follows should last less than a minute and should demonstrate the pair's understanding of how to create and sustain dramatic tension. To aid this, stipulate that the scene should have only two lines.

A [*high status*]. Why are you staring [or grinning]?

B [*low status*]. You'll never guess to who you're talking.

B's line must be the end of the scene.

Show the scenes to the rest of the class. Ask the audience to evaluate how dramatic tension was communicated and sustained: this will help them in their own pieces, as well as support this group's work. Also ask them to suggest who the characters might be. Where? When? As in other structures, this opens other possibilities for further exploration in Stage 2.

Next, play Nina Simone's version of 'Pirate Jenny' (available on iTunes). The lyrics follow. Distribute these lyrics while it is playing. Then ask each person for a question that is raised by the narrative/narrator that might subsequently be explored (and will be, in Stage 2). For instance:

- Who is she and why is she in the hotel (the backstory)?
- Why is the black freighter rescuing her now?
- Why is she so vengeful?
- Is what she describes real or a fantasy?

5. Ask the group to create a scene with a revenge-fantasy sequence, inspired by 'Pirate Jenny'. The scene must include clear conventions to establish the difference between reality and fantasy. Any words used must be taken from the lyrics of the song.

Famously, *The Threepenny Opera* is a socialist critique of capitalist society. However, it is important to ask the group to consider what the theme of their work might be. To facilitate this in preparation for Stage 2, ask them what themes emerge from their work on 'Pirate Jenny'. They are likely to suggest such possibilities as:

- Inequality
- Power struggle
- Oppression
- Revolution

'Pirate Jenny' (1928)
by Bertolt Brecht and Kurt Weill, translated by Marc Blitzstein

You people can watch while I'm scrubbing these floors
And I'm scrubbin the floors while you're gawking.
Maybe once ya tip me and it makes ya feel swell
In this crummy southern town
In this crummy old hotel
But you'll never guess to who you're talkin.
No. You couldn't ever guess to who you're talkin.
Then one night there's a scream in the night
And you'll wonder who could that have been?
And you see me kinda grinnin while I'm scrubbin
And you say, what's she got to grin?
I'll tell you.
There's a ship.
The black freighter
With a skull on its masthead
Will be coming in.
You gentlemen can say, 'Hey gal, finish them floors!
Get upstairs! What's wrong with you! Earn your keep here!'
You toss me your tips
And look out to the ships
But I'm counting your heads
As I'm making the beds
Cuz there's nobody gonna sleep here, honey.
Nobody – Nobody!
Then one night there's a scream in the night
And you say, 'Who's that kicking up a row?'

And ya see me kinda starin out the winda
And you say, 'What's she got to stare at now?'
I'll tell ya.
There's a ship,
The black freighter
Turns around in the harbour
Shootin guns from her bow.
Now you gentlemen can wipe off that smile off your face
Cause every building in town is a flat one.
This whole frickin place will be down to the ground.
Only this cheap hotel standing up safe and sound
And you yell, 'Why do they spare that one?'
Yes.
That's what you say.
'Why do they spare that one?'
All the night through, through the noise and to-do
You wonder who is that person that lives up there?
And you see me stepping out in the morning
Looking nice with a ribbon in my hair.
And the ship,
The black freighter
Runs a flag up its masthead
And a cheer rings the air.
By noontime the dock
Is a-swarmin with men
Comin out from the ghostly freighter.
They move in the shadows
Where no one can see
And they're chainin up people
And they're bringin em to me
Askin me,
'Kill them now, or later?'
Askin me!
'Kill them now, or later?'
Noon by the clock

And so still by the dock
You can hear a foghorn miles away.
And in that quiet of death
I'll say, 'Right now.
Right now!'
Then they'll pile up the bodies
And I'll say,
'That'll learn ya!'
And the ship,
The black freighter
Disappears out to sea
And
On – It – Is – Me

2. Selecting, Structuring and Developing

You now have a range of possibilities and directions in which to take the work. The group should discuss whether any of the various directions in which the work has spiralled could or should be linked up, or whether they wish to focus on a particular area.

- They might wish to take the conventions used in the play and apply them to a plot they devise on the same themes as the play.

- They might choose to focus on the character of Pirate Jenny, using one or more of the questions they raised in response to the song. Or, thinking laterally, they might want to research Nina Simone (1933–2003). Her life and her civil-rights activism explain the ferocity and intensity of her rendition of the song: clearly, what inspired her was her experience as a Black woman in a period of social injustice and oppression.

- They might want to use the 'spin-off' series principle and create a sequel or prequel – perhaps the early life and times of Mr and Mrs Peachum, or Filch's backstory. Or indeed, a story based around the mysterious black freighter.

- They might want to develop a longer piece based on their Activity 3 piece.

- They might use the montage principle (see Structure 3) and create a series of scenes on whatever they identify as the central theme.

- Or they might want to create a miniature version of *The Threepenny Opera*, using a combination of extracts from the script and their own versions of other scenes.

If the group use the techniques, conventions and form of *The Three-penny Opera* (or the play you have chosen), the question, 'How do you want to tell this story?' has, to some extent, been answered before the answer to 'What's the story you want to tell?' Similarly, given Brecht's didactic intention, the answers to the questions 'Why do you want to tell it?' and 'What effect do you want to have on the audience?' are clear. Nevertheless, these answers need to be demonstrated in performance, not merely understood in theory. Given the distancing effect that Brechtian techniques strive for, it is also worth applying Exercise 41 on moving from third person to first person (page 198) in Part 3.

3. Rehearsing

For general guidance on Stage 3 of the devising process, see pages 143–146.

Structure 9

Same Starting Point, Different Outcomes

Earlier in this book, I mentioned that it is possible to start the devising process before assigning final performance groups. In this structure, the generating and exploring stage is devoted to whole-class work, offering a range of activities in various groupings. This enables you not only to experiment with different possible performance groupings, to see how and if they gel, but also, given the different skills and attributes required for each activity, provides insight into the different strengths individual students may have.

Most of the other structures in this section of the book could be used in the same way. However, the theme of this structure has been chosen because it opens up a large number of interpretations and directions. It also deliberately collectivises the development stage so that groups may end up developing work in Stage 2 which others have originated in Stage 1. In this way, good ideas can be shared around.

The theme is *transformation*, be it personal, social or historical. The term also encompasses theatrical transformation, whether from one character to another or from one scene to another. In this way, the relationship between theme and content are inextricably linked in students' minds from the start of the process.

The activities in Stage 1 do not have to occur in the order below. They can be used in the sequence that best matches your class' previous experience and strengths.

1. Generating and Exploring

1. Divide the class into groups of four or five. Ask each group to discuss how people feel about change and record these feelings in a series of keywords. Resist the temptation to get bogged down in a discussion of whether the change in question is good or bad. Regardless, it is the process of change, rather than the reasons for or consequences of change that should be the focus of the discussion.

Using their list of keywords, ask the same groups to each create an abstract piece that expresses the process of change. Stipulate that no dialogue is allowed but sound and random words are permissible.

If your group is not used to working in non-naturalistic ways, ask each individual to work on a series of six movements, which are then repeated, with an accompanying sound. The juxtaposition of the individual activities within the group creates images and meaning for the audience to interpret. If necessary, suggest a sequence of movements – these could be taken from one of the movement sequences in Stage 1 of Structure 5: No Inspiration Required. Impose a couple of additional criteria – perhaps that the sequence must be repeated at different speeds and that there must be one point in the sequence where the whole group is physically connected in some way.

Each group then shows their piece to the whole class. The audience response will inform subsequent planning and the development of ideas. To maximise the usefulness of this, ensure that the audience know before they see the work that:

- Everyone in the audience must respond with a mood, an emotion, a narrative, a situation triggered by what they have seen.
- Everyone in the audience must express their views positively.

This activity will reveal who has an aptitude for abstract work and who is skilled at developing an idea from this sort of stimuli.

2. Rotate groups. By this I mean retain the same rehearsal group as for Activity 1, but assign each group the list of responses to another group's abstract piece. Ask each group to select one of the suggestions on their new list to develop into a scene. The scene should be:

- Naturalistic – although it should begin and end with the same frozen image.
- No more than one hundred words may be spoken in the scene. This is partly to push them in the direction of narrative economy and also to minimise the amount of time it will take to write the scene down as a script, which they need for later work.

Pay particular attention to:

- How the group negotiate and decide which option to choose.
- Which students know how to use forms of communication other than speech.
- Which students seem skilled at characterisation.

The scenes should be shown before they are written down, for possible inclusion in Stage 2.

3. A mystery always hooks the attention but, unless your group are all studying History – which seems unlikely – you will need to assign the stimulus for this activity at the end of the previous session, in order that students can research in the meantime.

> **Notice of Change of Name**
>
> From the *Stratford Gazette*, 20th March 1915
>
> I formally, wholly, absolutely and utterly renounce, relinquish and abandon the Christian and Surname of Carl Schneider.
>
> I declare that I have assumed, adopted and determined and I intend henceforth, upon all occasions whatsoever to use and sub-scribe myself by the name of Charles Bennett instead of Carl Schneider.
>
> Dated this 17th day of March 1915
>
> Charles Bennett (Formerly known as Carl Schneider)

Distribute this stimulus and ask the class to find out what might have been happening in March 1915 that led to this announcement. It makes their research slightly easier if you reveal that the Stratford in question is the subsequent home of the London Olympics, not the one on Avon. For your information, Carl Schneider, like many other German-born or British citizens whose family were of German origin, was a shopkeeper in Newham who changed his name in wake of anti-German riots during the First World War.

Once the whole class have shared their research findings, assign new groups, again of four or five. Ask each group to create a scene showing an event leading up to the decision, utilising what they know about communicating tension.

Show the resulting scenes and take note of who knows how to construct scenes to create tension: that is, has an eye for the effect on the audience. Of course, the quality of research, and whether it has been done at all, will indicate which groups have research interests and abilities.

4. As a whole-class activity, ask students, individually and simultaneously, to make a spontaneous solo image of 'The Hero'. Give them a countdown. They shouldn't need more than ten seconds. Ask three or four of the class to hold their poses while the rest identify what it is about stance, expression and gesture that indicate a hero?

Next, ask the whole class to make spontaneous solo images of 'The Villain'. Again, ask three or four of the class to hold their poses while the rest identify what it is about stance, expression and gesture that indicate a villain?

Next, assign groups for the rest of this activity, in different combinations from the groups assigned for Activities 1 to 3. Ask the group to create a still picture called 'The Terrorists'. Give them a minute or so. Ensure they can remember their picture for long enough to show it after they have been assigned and made the second group still image: 'The Freedom Fighters'. Ask half the groups to show one or other picture first, then the other, to the rest of the class. Then reverse so that the audience become the performers and vice versa.

Discuss and evaluate how you tell the difference. Someone is likely to articulate the fact that the titles are interchangeable, depending on whose side you are on and who has the power to name and define. However, if no one does, you should.

In the same groups, ask students to discuss and note circumstances in which people change their name. Their list should include willing and formal changes of name (such as on marriage), situations when the surname or a number takes over from the forename (prison or army), those names which are associated with a role in your life (such as teachers called Sir or Miss; parents called Mum or Dad); people changing their names or having them changed – many immigrants arriving in the USA at Ellis Island had their names anglicised by immigration officials. Many Jewish refugees did the same when they arrived in the UK, to avoid further persecution. You may also wish to include names bestowed by those intending to demean a person because of her or his gender, sexuality or race. If so, make clear your ground rules regarding what language is permissible.

Subdivide the group into pairs (or a pair and a trio). Ask each pair to create a monologue for a character whose name has been changed, for one of the reasons outlined in the previous paragraph. While the monologue should focus on the effect that has had on the person, they should consider who is being addressed and what is expressed through words and what emerges through subtext, eye line and so forth.

5. This activity uses Martin Luther King's 'I have a dream' speech as the stimulus for work which uses physical transformation, and so unites form and content. Martin Luther King (1929–1968) was one of the great orators of the twentieth century. The speech, which can be found online, was designed to be spoken so it should be read aloud. Neutrally. Attempting to emulate his delivery would be counterproductive. (I suggest one clause or sentence a time around the circle as a whole class. I also suggest beginning towards the end of an extremely long speech, with the line 'Let us not wallow in the valley of despair'.)

Deliberately, the activity does not require prior historical knowledge of Martin Luther King or the civil-rights movement. You might want to ask if the class know who the speaker was and what the time and context was, but it is not vital at this stage. If you wish, the earlier part of the speech will provide a bit more context.

Ask everyone to choose a line or image from the speech that inspires them, moves them, captures their imagination in some way. You might wish to assign groups on the basis of who has responded to which line. However they are assigned, each group should create a 'before' frozen image of the world that Martin Luther King is describing. Encourage the group to think of an abstract representation rather than a literal dramatisation of a line from the speech, although either is usable.

One by one, each person should step out of the group to look at the whole image and adjust one aspect of it, to heighten the effect. They then resume their position. Someone else steps out to further heighten the effect until everyone has done so.

In the same groups, create an 'after' image, having remembered or recorded their 'before' image position in some way so that it can be revisited later in this activity.

Next, the group should resume their 'before' position. Assign someone in each group – or let the group decide the best person – to count down from ten to indicate the move from 'before' to 'after'. The transformation must be timed to last the full ten beats of the count. Repeat once or twice so that the transformation can be as fluid as possible. The counter remains in the group – they just have to be able to move and count at the same time.

Ask each group to demonstrate another way that they could create the transformation, such as a count of five or a count of two, or building and deconstructing the image one person at a time, or moving away then back together simultaneously.

2. Selecting, Structuring and Developing

I recommend that, before assigning final rehearsal groups, you ask students to reflect, individually, on which of the possible themes and directions most captures their imaginations, or rank the possibilities in order of preference. This can then be used as a factor in determining who should work with whom.

Different themes and directions to suggest to the groups include:

- A montage-style piece, inspired by Activity 1 but incorporating ideas and suggestions from Activity 2, on the process of change.
- A more naturalistic piece, taking one of the narratives suggested in response to Activity 1 and incorporating one of the scenes developed in Activity 2.
- The story of Carl Schneider/Charles Bennett, as explored in Activity 3.
- A multiple-protagonist narrative, on the theme of 'the power to name is the power to define', developing work from Activity 4.
- A piece contrasting then and now, perhaps focusing on the civil-rights movement, but certainly incorporating the transformation techniques used in Activity 5.

You will more than likely have your own suggestions and possibilities that emerge from the work the whole class has done.

If a group want to develop Activity 4 work, I recommend you give them the poem 'Each Man Has A Name' by Zelda Mishkovsky, which can be found online.

If a group want to develop Activity 5 work, you may wish to provide iconic images which could be incorporated into the work. I have used the famous photo of Tommie Smith and John Carlos's Black Power salute on the medals podium at the 1968 Mexico Olympics for this. Also, encourage research into other campaigners for social transformation, such as Sojourner Truth, Rosa Parks, Malcolm X and Barack Obama. Their words are far more eloquent than anything you or I or our students could come up with.

Regardless of which direction the group take, the key questions should be borne in mind and student resource sheets 1 and 3 (pages 147 and 149) should be used to ensure that your candidates create characters with sufficient depth and detail. Exercises regarding characterisation from Part 3: Refining, Troubleshooting and Finishing can also be assigned as part of this stage of the devising process, as required.

3. Rehearsing

For general guidance on Stage 3 of the devising process, see pages 143–146.

No Feeling, No Emotion

This structure is designed for boys' groups, in particular the types of boys who were the subject of concern in the Question 6 in Part 1 of this book. This structure explores the My Lai massacre. This infamous episode in the Vietnam War occurred on 16th March 1968, when the US soldiers of Charlie Company, under the command of Lieutenant William Calley, entered a Vietnamese village and massacred over three hundred apparently unarmed civilians including women, children and the elderly. In this way, the structure uses aspects of war as a vehicle to explore aspects of masculinity and areas of concern in your students' own lives: bravery, being judged and found wanting, family responsibilities, peer pressure or the responsibility of the witness.

Each activity in Stage 1 offers a highly structured series of short tasks. Overall, Stage 1 is designed to provide strategies which are proven to help boys to engage and attain, such as:

- Detective work, as a means of hooking and engaging the attention of the group. For this reason, it is important that My Lai is not referred to before the point specified in Stage 1.
- A safety net, wherein these issues can be explored without the group, individually or collectively, feeling exposed and vulnerable.
- Work that is physically based but which is scaffolded in ways that temper exuberance with control.

1. Generating and Exploring

1. According to the American Army manual, 'drill is the foundation of discipline in battle'. So military drill is an appropriate place to begin. In preparation for this, the group should list the type of situations where a man might have to present a brave or confident exterior, despite feeling anything but brave or confident on the inside.

Ask them to create two still images that represent first the exterior and then the interior. Their list of such situations should be retained for Stage 2 and they should find some way of recording or remembering these solo images, for use later in this activity.

Next, ask them to list – and research if necessary – the commands that are used in military drill. If it makes your life easier, simply assign them the following list.

- Attention.
- Present arms.
- Shoulder arms.
- Stand at ease.
- Right turn (or left turn).
- Quick march.
- At ease.
- Fall out.

First, they should create a group of soldiers on parade. You may choose the most obvious sergeant major in the group, or the least likely candidate. Or allow the group to select. Whoever is chosen, he should drill the group so that the movements are precise and take place in unison.

Once the drill has been established, the group should work out a moment where the action freezes and all the soldiers, including the sergeant major, transform into the still image they created earlier which expresses the interior state. They should experiment with how this transformation occurs. Perhaps it is a slow dissolve in and out of the still image, in which case, how long does it take? Perhaps it begins with a convulsive move, as if the body is being taken over. It is worth playing around with freezing the drill action at different points, so that one or two transform into and out of the inner state, with sufficient points for all the group to transform.

2. For this activity, give the group the following quote:

I gave them a good boy and they made him a murderer.

Do not provide any context at this stage. One of the group is assigned or volunteers to be the good boy who became a murderer. This does not require anything more than sitting in a chair in the centre of a circle (as large as possible) formed by the rest of the group. The circle becomes the walls of the cell where the former good boy is imprisoned: whether he is on remand or has been convicted and sentenced need not be addressed at this point. One by one, the rest of the group take on the role of a parent or brother. One by one, they enter the cell. No words should be spoken in the interaction: the visitor should convey their feelings non-verbally. (If you think the visitor's response might be violent, stipulate that there must be no physical contact with the prisoner.) The prisoner should respond appropriately. The scene should last thirty seconds. (Get one of the group to time it.) As the family member is about to exit, he turns and addresses a single line to the prisoner. That line might be supportive or reassuring. It might be an expression of the anger or shame the family member feels. It might be incoherent or uncomprehending of how he and they come to be in this situation. There is no right or wrong beyond the need to relate to the tone and quality of the interaction in the scene.

A record should be kept of the lines spoken and of the possibilities that the group come up with when asked, after the scene, to speculate:

- Who might the 'good boy' be?
- Who might the 'they' referred to be?
- What might have occurred? (A murder, evidently, but for what reasons and in what circumstances?)

3. Place a chair in the centre of the group's circle. Ask one of them to volunteer to embody a man with a tremor, unable to make eye contact, clearly on medication, who keeps his house like a fortress and never goes out. The rest of the group should advise and demonstrate to the volunteer how all the above can be communicated, without speech and without the presence of anyone else in the scene. To make life easier, the volunteer is allowed to stand and move a maximum of three times, although he should return to the chair after each move.

Once the routine has been established, place chairs in a row, one for each member of the group. They should recreate the sequence they have built, in unison. In effect, this creates a multiple image of the man in the self-imposed fortress. This may take some time to rehearse.

Now, pick one of the members of the group: it needs to be someone with good sight-reading skills. Give him the sheet containing Varnardo Simpson's testimony. Varnardo Simpson was one of the soldiers who participated in the massacre. It is from his testimony that the title of this structure is taken. The speaker should not show the testimony to the rest of the group. (But he should be briefed that My Lai is pronounces 'me-lie'.) He should stand behind the line of chairs and read it aloud, as they go through their movement sequence again. If the sequence finishes before the testimony, it should be repeated.

My Lai: Varnardo Simpson's Account

That day in My Lai, I was personally responsible for killing about twenty-five people. Personally. Men, women. From shooting them, to cutting their throats, scalping them, to . . . cutting off their hands and cutting out their tongues. I did it.

I just went. My mind just went. And I wasn't the only one that did it. A lot of other people did it. I just killed. Once I started, the – the training, the whole programming part of killing, it just came out.

A lot of people were doing it. I just followed suit. I just lost all sense of direction, of purpose. I just started killing any kinda way I could kill. It just came. I didn't know I had it in me.

> After I killed the child, my whole mind just went. It just went. And once you start, it's very easy to keep on. Once you start. The hardest – the part that's hard is to kill, but once you kill, that becomes easier, to kill the next person and the next one and the next one. Because I had no feelings and no emotions or no nothing. No direction. I just killed.

4. Every group with whom I have used the testimony has found it hard to keep going with the sequence, such is its impact. Every group has wanted to know if the words are true and what or where is My Lai? This is the point for them to find out.

There are numerous accounts of the massacre and its aftermath. The best is the 1989 documentary *Four Hours in My Lai* which can, at the time of writing, be viewed on YouTube (second-hand copies can be found on VHS too). To whet their appetites – and also because it is true! – I suggest you forewarn the group that they may find what is described and seen very distressing. For this reason, I also suggest that you watch it yourself, in advance, in case there is anything that your school or college would find inappropriate to be shown in lesson time. There is also a book, with the same title, by Michael Bilton and Kevin Sim, from where the quotes on the resource sheets for this structure are taken, although all the testimony is spoken in the documentary too.

The group should discuss their feelings, and write down their individual response to what they have seen and learned about My Lai and Vietnam. They should also write down the questions that this raises for them. These notes should be retained for Stage 2 of their devising process.

5. Tell the group that they are going to create a movement sequence that represents the My Lai massacre. They are all GIs. None of them are villagers. To avoid pandemonium, build the sequence in the following steps.

a) Individually, each person creates four solo still images, each of which represents a moment in the GIs' time in My Lai. They may choose to incorporate earlier movements from the drill sequence or the interior state from Activity 1.

b)   Next, they should identify four different places to stand, one for each of the still images. They should practice moving, in slow motion, from one place to another, holding each still image for five seconds.

c)   Introduce a piece of music to heighten the atmosphere. It could either be something beautiful and poignant which provides an ironic counterpoint – Albinoni's 'Adagio' was used to great effect in the film *Gallipoli*. Or it could be something discordant and harsh: a lot of dubstep would work. Alternately, individuals in the group could bring in music. Several options, with contrasting effects, can only be beneficial to the work.

d)   Finally, introduce the second resource sheet of testimony. Ask the group to decide the best way of incorporating some of the quotations. They could be spoken by those in the movement sequence or one or more of the group could step out of the action to speak them. They should also experiment with overlapping dialogue, creating a montage of sound. If they have the necessary technical skills, they could be recorded as voice-overs and mixed in with the music that is being used to accompany the sequence.

My Lai: Testimony

'I gave them a good boy and they made him a murderer.'
GI's mother

'We had orders, but the orders we had was that we were going into an enemy village and that they was well armed. I didn't find that when I got there. And ordering me to shoot down innocent people, that's not an order – that's craziness to me, you know. And so I don't feel like I have to obey that.'
Harry Stanley, Charlie Company

'We were kids, eighteen, nineteen years old. I was twenty-one years old at the time. I was one of the oldest people around there among the common grunts.

Most of them [Charlie Company] had never been away from home before they went into the service. And they end up in Vietnam, many of them because they thought they were going to do something courageous on behalf of their country. Here are these guys who have gone in and in a moment, in a moment, following orders, in a context in which they'd been trained, prepared to follow orders, they do what they're told, and they shouldn't have, and they look back a day later and realise they probably made the biggest mistake of their lives. [There were] only a few extraordinary people who were in those circumstances who had the presence of mind and strength of their own character that would see them through. Most people didn't. And for most of them – people that I was personally just stunned to discover had made the wrong choice they did – they all had to live with it. They had to live with it. And so do we all.'

Ronald Ridenhour, GI not with Charlie Company

'When my troops were getting massacred and mauled by an enemy I couldn't see, I couldn't feel and I couldn't touch, nobody in the military system ever described them as anything other than Communism. They didn't give it a race, they didn't give it a sex, they didn't give it an age. They never let me believe it was just a philosophy in a man's mind that was my enemy out there.'

Lt William Calley's final speech to his court martial

'I think of it all the time, and that is why I am old before my time. I remember it all the time. I think about it and I can't sleep. I'm all alone and life is hard and there's no one I can turn to for help. Then I think of it all the time. I'm always sad and unhappy, and that's why I'm old.

I think of my daughter and my mother, both of them dead. I won't forgive. I hate them very much. I won't forgive them as long as I live. Think of those children, that small . . . Those children still at

their mothers' breasts being killed . . . I hate them very much . . . I miss my mother, my sister, my children. I think of them lying dead. I think of it and feel my insides being cut to pieces.'
Truong Thi Lee, who lost nine members of her family in the massacre

2. Selecting, Structuring and Developing

You now have several fully developed movement sequences, which could either be incorporated into the piece or could function as a linking or framing device. In order to decide the focus and direction that their work takes from here, the group should review:

- The reasons they gave in Activity 1 that a man might have to present a brave and confident exterior.
- The possibilities they imagined for the good boy who became a murderer in Activity 2.
- Their responses to watching *Four Hours in My Lai* and the questions this raised – do any of these form the basis for development?

While the group might want to produce a piece about the My Lai massacre and its aftermath, they may also want to consider using one of the following themes as the basis for their piece, placed in a parallel context.

- Taking a stand or saying 'No' despite pressure not to do so.
- Following orders.
- Responsibility of the witness (such as the photographer).

A couple of other points and alternate possibilities:

1. Watching *Four Hours in My Lai*, it is impossible to miss the disproportionate number of African-Americans who served in Vietnam and were involved in the My Lai massacre. In 1967, Mohammed Ali was

stripped of his world heavyweight title for refusing to be conscripted. As he said at the time:

'Why should they ask me to put on a uniform and go 10,000 miles from home and drop bombs and bullets on brown people in Vietnam while so-called Negro people in Louisville are treated like dogs and denied simple human rights? No, I'm not going 10,000 miles from home to help murder and burn another poor nation simply to continue the domination of white slave masters of the darker people the world over. This is the day when such evils must come to an end.'

This quote could be used if the groups want to locate the piece in a broader social context.

By the way, although the work concerns American soldiers, I urge that no American accents need be attempted: it is the universality of the theme and the situation that is the point, not a student's dialect ability.

2. If the group want to explore a parallel situation, ask them to research Private Harry Farr. He was one of over three hundred British soldiers who were court-martialled and shot for desertion or cowardice during the First World War. It is now acknowledged that this behaviour was caused by shell shock or post-traumatic stress disorder. The soldiers were posthumously pardoned, ninety years later, in 2006. Alan Bleasdale's TV series, *The Monocled Mutineer*, featured a scene where the title character had to guard a young soldier the night before the latter was shot for desertion. It's heartbreaking.

If you want to incorporate scenes from plays about war into the group's piece, you – and they – are spoilt for choice. Apart from the obvious ones – *Oh! What a Lovely War* (1961), *Journey's End* (1928), *The Long, the Short and the Tall* (1959), *The Accrington Pals* (1982) – several American playwrights have written plays based on the experience of Vietnam. David Rabe wrote a trilogy based on his experience of being drafted: *Sticks and Bones* (1969), *The Basic Training of Pavlo Hummel* (1971) and *Streamers* (1976).

You will note that the key questions that are posed on student resource sheet 2 (page 148) and elsewhere have, to some extent, begun to be answered because of the forms and conventions used in Stage 1 of the process. Nevertheless, the group still need to consider the story they want to tell and why they want to tell it, as well as the effect they want to have on the audience.

Regardless of which direction the group take, student resource sheets 1 and 3 (pages 147 and 149) should be used to ensure that your candidates create characters with sufficient depth and detail. Exercises regarding characterisation from Part 3: Refining, Troubleshooting and Finishing can also be assigned as part of this stage of the devising process, as required.

Finally, given the need for boys to have greater structure to scaffold their work, the more criteria you impose for them, the better! I suggest the following:

- The piece should move backwards and forwards in time.
- The piece should feature at least two 30-second sequences with no dialogue.
- The piece should feature a chorus, commenting on events.
- The piece should feature an abstract sequence, which communicates the emotional effect of events on the relatives of the My Lai villagers, or a relative of an executed soldier.

However, you are the best judge of what is required to help shape their work and to maintain their focus and engagement.

3. Rehearsing

For general guidance on Stage 3 of the devising process, see page 143–146.

An Overview of Stage 3: Rehearsing

As I wrote in the introduction to this part of the book, the third stage of a devising rehearsal process should be about reworking and revisiting, refining, editing, honing, discarding, paring down and polishing. The guiding principle for this stage is simple: *Do it again, make it better!*

From the teacher's point of view, overseeing the devising process, Stage 3 is about refining the material and the performances, troubleshooting problems and guiding towards the all-important finishing touches. That is why Part 3 of this book focuses on this aspect of your task.

From my vantage point – and based on my experience – regardless of the group, the stimulus, and the form, content and style of the piece being devised, there are various general points which must always be monitored in the final stage of the devising process. These are:

- Does the piece have a structure that works for the theme, content and form?

- Are the theatrical conventions and techniques used in the piece appropriate and consistent?

- Is there narrative economy and clarity?

- Are they telling us through dialogue what they should be showing us through action?

- Will the audience want to know what happens next? We don't need to know who the characters are from the outset, or where they are, but we do need to want to find out more.

- Do scenes outstay their welcome?
- What is the intended effect on the audience: scene by scene, sequence by sequence, as well as overall? Is that effect being achieved?
- Are they rushing? Do the audience have time to register characters, relationships, atmosphere, key plot points?
- Is there too much plot? If so, it is likely to lack depth and detail.
- What is the running time? This needs to be monitored throughout the process, to ensure that it is within whatever length is stipulated by your exam specification.
- Is each performer realising their full potential? If not, why not? In particular, is someone else in the group preventing this?

I refer you to the questions posed in Part 3: Refining, Troubleshooting and Finishing for specific solutions to specific problems.

The better Drama teachers I know also ensure that students return to and review the assessment criteria just before exam, to double-check that they are demonstrating all that they need to, to maximise their attainment.

It is crucial that, as the date of performance looms, each group gets used to running their piece without stopping. Once again, I apologise if this seems like a statement of the obvious. I have seen far too many pieces where it is clear that this did not happen with sufficient frequency or at all during the process. To prepare groups for this, schedule time to watch each group in a stop-start run. Make it clear that you are the one who decides whether they need to stop and start and why! Next, allocate a time for you to watch a runthrough by each group where you give notes, like a director, at the end.

It is also important to acknowledge that running out of steam is often part of the process, particularly in Stage 3. It happens to the best of us. Energy and inspiration desert us. The activities in the opening stage of Structure 5: No Inspiration Required can be appropriated and assigned for a group who need to be revitalised and got on their feet and doing something, anything. Here are some other possible activities. They're fun: sometimes, in the intensity of the devising rehearsal process, it helps to be reminded that making theatre is meant to be challenging, exciting, demanding, rigorous – but it's also meant to be enjoyable.

The first three exercises can be used as whole-class warm-ups, as well as assigned to individual groups. All were taught me by writers, as ways of reawakening creativity when they felt blocked. All are spontaneous improvisation exercises.

1. First, the class or group walk around the studio at a brisk pace, pointing (with arm fully extended, rather than vaguely indicating) at an object and naming it, in a loud clear tone. 'Wall', 'Chair', 'Poster', 'Whiteboard.' Whatever they can see. Give them a minute – everyone should be able to name at least ten objects in that time.

Next, ask them walk again, and point again, and name again. However, this time, they must call the object anything other than what it actually is. So, the same four objects might be, 'Kangaroo', 'Tomato', 'Switzerland', 'Multi-storey car park'. It's surprisingly hard to do: the mind goes blank. But names (or misnames) will come and that, somehow, sets the creative juices flowing.

2. In pairs, on the floor, with a real or imaginary box. A pulls out an imaginary object and names it. For instance, 'Oh look, it's a fur coat.' B adds a detail: 'Yes, and it's moth-eaten.' A throws that object to one side and pulls out another object. The ease or lack of it with which the object is removed should indicate what size and shape and whether it's resistant (it might be, if it's animate). Reverse, when A begins to run out of steam so that B pulls the object out and A adds the detail.

3. The class or group sit in a circle. A mimes an activity. B asks, 'What are you doing?' A describes any activity except what they are doing. B then starts miming the activity that A has described. A then asks B 'What are you doing?' B describes any activity except what they are doing. A then starts miming that activity. Continue until one or other pauses too long or names an activity that has been named or names an activity too similar to the one being mimed. In which case, another

person takes over. The pace should be rapid. It doesn't have to go round the circle in sequence: people can step back in as soon as they wish. However, everyone in the circle must participate at least once. Apart from awakening creativity, it's also useful for overcoming fear of failure. Everyone freezes, physically or vocally. Nothing bad actually happens!

4. In 1975, the musician and conceptual artist Brian Eno created a deck of printed cards called Oblique Strategies. Each card offers an aphorism intended to help artists, particularly musicians, break creative blocks by encouraging lateral thinking. (Sets of these cards are available for purchase online, if you're interested.) The principle, then, is the same as the counterintuitive suggestions referred to earlier. So you might suggest playing a sad scene as a hilarious comedy or a quiet introspective scene as a loud, furious slanging match. Whatever reawakens interest in the work!

To get as high a mark a possible you need to create characters who are:

- Convincing and believable.

- Different from each other, if you play more than one character.

Most people are better at playing certain types of character than others. For instance, some people are more convincing in high-status roles and some are better at low-status characters. Professional actors are often 'typecast'. This means they usually play the romantic lead or the villain or someone very posh. Some people enjoy playing a 'baddie'. Some people are good at playing characters much older or younger than they are in real life. Ask yourself and the others in your group:

- What are my strengths and weaknesses?

Play to your strengths when you can, but also push yourself outside your comfort zone when you need to.

Remember:

- Use what you know about how different people behave, talk and react in real life to make sure that the characters and relationships you create are believable.

- How people move, stand and sit reveals a great deal about their mood, situation and feelings.

- What people say and don't say, as well as how they say it or don't, reveals a great deal about who they are and who they are with.

- No matter how different a character is from you, there is always something that has happened to you that will enable you to connect with what the character is experiencing.

Some forms of theatre require big gestures and exaggerated ways of moving and speaking. Depending on the style of your piece, you may be playing larger-than-life characters – but they still need to be based on truthful, recognisable human beings.

As rehearsals progress, use student resource sheet 3 to develop more depth, more detail – and gain more marks!

Don't fall into the trap of working out plot in advance. That won't gain high marks because, in this exam, it's not the story you tell, it's the way that you tell it!

So, if you want to get the highest possible marks, don't just ask yourself:

- **What's the story we want to tell?**

You should also ask yourself:

- **How do we want to tell this story?**
- **Why do we want to tell this story?**
- **What effect do we want to have on the audience?**

Why? Because your piece will be assessed on the way that plot, theme, style and form come together, and how effectively you communicate with an audience.

Here are some other important questions to ask at the start of your devising process:

What makes a good beginning?

- There is no single right way to begin – grabbing the audience's attention is what counts. The audience don't need to know who the characters are from the outset, or where they are, but we do need to want to find out more.
- With a partner, make notes or discuss a play, film or TV programme you have seen where the opening made you want to keep watching. Why did it do so?

How will our play be structured?

- Sometimes the action takes place as a continuous narrative. This is known as linear structure.
- Sometimes a play uses moves backwards and forwards in time.
- Sometimes a play begins at the end of the story, and then flashes back to the start of the story, to follow events through and explain what happened.
- Some plays are a series of interconnected stories or scenes on a particular theme.

There are many different **narrative structures**. None are right or wrong but some are more appropriate than others, depending on how you want to tell your story.

Make sure you know what the following terms mean so that you can use them.

- **Three-act structure / Cliffhanger / Dramatic irony / Climax and anticlimax / Contrast**

Your group also needs to consider:

- **What do you know about different styles and theatrical genres?**
- **Does your story fit into a particular genre?**

Also, list all the **techniques** and **conventions** you have learned about different ways to communicate to an audience. You don't need to use them all in your piece – but which will you use to tell your story in the most effective way?

The audience doesn't need to be told everything about a character's background. But *you* need to know! The more you know, the greater the depth and detail you will bring to your characterisation – and the higher the mark. Here are some things that you will need to know about the character(s) you are playing. There maybe other things you want to add.

- Gender and exact age.
- Body language, walk, gestures, posture and mannerisms.
- Personal history: home, family, social background, past experience.
- Relationships with others, especially status.
- Voice and vocabulary.
- Strengths and weaknesses; hopes and fears.

These questions are based on the work of Konstantin Stanislavsky (1863–1938), who created a system that he hoped would lead to a truthful style of acting.

1. Who am I?

All that you have imagined and decided about your character, or, if your piece is based on a true story, all the facts you know about that character.

2. Where am I?

Alone or with other people? In a quiet or a noisy place? Is this a familiar place where you feel comfortable or a strange, even hostile environment? Inside or outdoors?

3. When is it?

Not just time of day, not just time of year, but which year?

4. Where have I just come from?

What has happened to the character immediately before the scene starts? How has it affected them?

5. What do I want?

Do you want something from the other person in the scene? Are you happy with your situation? Do you want to change it? Why do you want it? Why do you want it now?

Will it make your day or your whole life better? Do you need whatever it is desperately, to keep yourself alive?

6. What will happen if I don't get it now?

How will you get what you want? What must you overcome?

Remember to:

- Keep asking yourself these questions as your character(s) develop. The more you discover, the more likely it is your answers will change, develop and evolve.
- Think about how what happens to your character(s) during the course of the play changes and affects them. How will you communicate this to the audience?

To gain the highest possible marks, bear in mind the following tips and pitfalls throughout your devising rehearsal process:

- Rehearsal is reworking. It is very different to just working on a scene and showing it in a single lesson. Rehearsal involves revisiting, refining, editing, honing, discarding, paring down and polishing. In other words, doing it again and again, until it's as good as it possibly can be!

- As your piece develops, you might decide that there is a better place to begin than you thought originally. You will not know whether that's the best beginning from the start of your devising process.

- *Show* don't *tell*. Reveal through action, behaviour, body language and expression. Don't have characters tell us what they wouldn't actually say. For example, in real life, most people don't say, 'I'm angry.' They show they are angry by how they move, their tone of voice, etc.

- Is the effect you want to have on the audience clear? (Scene by scene, and sequence by sequence, as well as overall.) And what is that effect? Do you want to make them think about the world we live in? Make them sympathise with one character or angry with another? Do you want to create a tense or scary atmosphere that will have the audience on the edge of their seats? Do you want to move them to tears?

- Don't have too much plot! It will mean you are not working in the depth and detail you need to maximise your marks.

- Don't rush. Give the audience time to register characters, relationships, atmosphere, key plot points.

- A performance needs energy: volume and commitment are required, even in rehearsal.

- Avoid blackouts and avoid too many scene changes – marks are available for how you incorporate the transitions from scene to scene.

- Know your assessment criteria. What do you have to show in your work? Are you showing it?

- Is your piece the right length? Keep checking as you rehearse so that you don't have to cut out whole sections or extend other parts at the last minute.

Part Three

REFINING, TROUBLESHOOTING AND FINISHING

Overview

The ten structures in Part 2 of this book offer opportunities for students to respond to stimulus and to create engaging and effective pieces of theatre. Yet, as anyone who has managed the devising process a few times or examined student Drama knows, it is the degree of depth and detail, and the finishing touches which make a competent piece into a good one or a good piece into a great one. This part, Refining, Troubleshooting and Finishing, has two purposes. The first is to provide students with the means to ensure that, so far as is possible, they are able to create that depth and detail. The second is to enable you to step back, to ask yourself what's working and what's not, and to intervene accordingly and effectively.

It is worth reminding ourselves at this stage what an examiner is looking for. It's also worth noting that, in Drama, students are assessed both on their individual performances and their collective work. If Part 2: Making was concerned primarily with the latter, Part 3: Refining, Troubleshooting and Finishing focuses, although not exclusively, on the former.

Assessment criteria and the vocabulary used to describe them vary, depending on which specification you are following. However, the underlying concepts are the same. To attain the highest possible marks, it is important that your students demonstrate the following in their devised work:

Voice and movement

This includes:

- Clarity, control, pace, pitch, pause, projection, intonation, inflexion, rhythm.
- Physicalisation: movement (from naturalistic to abstract), gesture, expression, use of space and physical relationships (proxemics).

Working in role, creating a believable character or characters

This includes:

- Vocabulary, status, creating a backstory, versatility (if playing multiple roles), empathy (not commenting on the character, unless the theatrical form used requires that distance).

The relationship between style, content and form

Consideration of the overarching issues regarding style, content and form is built into the structures in Part 2. So, in this section, the emphasis is on such aspects as:

- Staging/visibility.
- Transitions between scenes.
- Performance conventions.

Communication within the ensemble and between performers and audience

This includes:

- Listening and responding to, and interacting with, each other.
- The intended effect on the audience and the extent to which that intention is achieved in performance.

You might reasonably ask why exam boards tend to separate voice and movement from the creation of character? You might point out, equally reasonably, that surely communication involves voice? Indeed. Such divisions are, to a great extent, artificial and created for assessment purposes, although some of the skills required are technical and mechanical – for instance, those categorised as voice and movement – while others are to do with the imaginative and the visceral – those characterised as working in role.

You can frazzle yourself to the point of frenzy by trying to separate out the assessment criteria and to map how the class are doing in relation to each assessment strand, individually and collectively. Why bother? That way lies exhaustion and nervous collapse. Experience has taught me that, essentially, we need to focus on two strands, both of which encompass both technical skills and creative choices.

- We need to ensure that our students *characterise* and all which that comprises.
- We need to ensure that our students *communicate*: within the ensemble and with the audience – and communication with the audience extends to and includes communication of story, style and form.

'Hold on!' I hear you cry. 'What about abstract work?' My argument is that the more extreme, heightened or stylised a piece is, the greater the needs for it to be rooted in something recognisable and true. In other words, human behaviour – or characterisation. Surely abstract work also requires a purpose that is clearly communicated within the ensemble and between the ensemble and audience? Otherwise we are just watching arms waving, or a quasi-expressionistic routine where the protagonist is circled to show the pressure they are under.

So, for the purposes of this section, I have identified what I have noticed to be the most common problems and suggested ways of addressing them, in a series of 'stand-alone' exercises, tips and suggestions, and organising them under these two main headings of *Characterisation* and *Communication*. For reasons that are explained in the sections themselves, each of these is preceded by short sections on the technical aspects of voice (*Audibility*) and staging (*Visibility*).

These exercises can be used in various ways and at various points in your rehearsal process, depending on your needs. Some of the exercises could and should eventually be incorporated into your earlier curriculum (see Question 3 in Part 1: Preparation), in order that your students have the necessary knowledge, skills and understanding *before* they begin their exam preparation. Some can be applied as a teacher-led, whole-group demonstration and modelling activity at the start of a rehearsal session. Some can be assigned, in the second or third stage of the devising process, depending on how far a scene or a character has been developed. What is required for one rehearsal group may not be appropriate for another. Some of the exercises are usually used by directors and actors working on a script, but have been adapted here for devised work.

I imagine that many of the exercises will be familiar to you already. The point is how to apply them strategically. To support this strategic, troubleshooting approach, and for ease of reference, I pose a question at the start of each exercise or series of exercises: Does the group or individual do A? In which case try B. Are the group or individual failing to do X? In which case, try Y. If the answer is 'Yes', then apply the exercise. If you're anything like me, there comes a point – approximately two-thirds of the way through the process, regular as clockwork in my case – when you can't see the wood for the trees. I hope that this approach and these questions will enable you to rediscover the leaves, branches and trunks, as it were. Regardless of which exercises you choose to use, the overarching aim is to maximise attainment by creating the best possible pieces of theatre.

1. Audibility

Can you hear them?

Voice is fundamentally important. Yet, often we neglect it. I suspect this is partly because we don't want to be seen as elocution teachers, denigrating our student with the tacit suggestion that 'How you talk now is wrong'. Less nobly, I suspect too that we tend to avoid voice work because, initially at least, it provokes embarrassment and self-consciousness. We all know that embarrassed or self-conscious students will tend to act out or sabotage the activity. Persevere. It is necessary. For audibility and clarity are vital in performance, regardless of the performer's own accent. Audibility and clarity are not the same thing: I know many loud but indistinct students. I am sure you do too.

When a person – on stage or off – is inaudible or indistinct, it is usually down to two things:

- They doubt their right to speak or lack confidence in what they are saying and in their ideas and opinions.
- They don't have the technical expertise to support what they are saying.

The advice in Part 1: Preparation and the three-stage devising process outlined in Part 2: Making should help build confidence. The following exercises address that lack of technical expertise.

Regular use of the activities in this section will improve your students' ability to speak with confidence and in character, whatever character is being played. A group, a scene, an individual speech may require specific technical voice work, in which case these exercises can be applied. However, most of the exercises in the following section can – and probably should – be done with most students. I recommend a whole-group vocal warm-up, comprised of the first three exercises, as a regular whole-group starter to your rehearsal sessions. Certainly, these exercises should be integrated into the entire process, rather than bolted on, in panic, at the last moment.

By the way, if any of your students are also singers, encourage them to incorporate what they know about voice production into their acting work, and to share their expertise with their group.

Exercise 1: Breathing

The most important muscle for an actor is the diaphragm, between the chest and the abdomen. This exercise works the muscles that support the voice and breathing so that the actor can control their voice and make it do what they want on stage.

1. Ask students to stand with their feet as wide apart as their hips and with their knees unlocked. (This stops the body from tensing up and, incidentally, is a good thing to do just before going on stage, particularly if the student is feeling nervous.) Students may wish to close their eyes to help concentration and minimise self-consciousness. Ask them to place their hands on their lower belly then breathe in slowly to a count of five. They should focus on feeling their chest cavity expand as the air fills it. Hold for a count of five. Now breathe out on the same count. Repeat this several times until they establish a rhythm. Do the same for a count of ten. Next – if they can – for a count of fifteen. Begin with you counting out loud: eventually the students should count silently on their own.

2. Ask students to breathe in. They should hum as they breathe out then open the mouth. The sound will become an 'aah'. Repeat a few times, varying the pitch each time.

3. The next step is to apply this to a speech. It could be a speech from their devised piece or, if there is nothing of suitable length or if such things have yet to be finalised, it can be applied to any monologue or poem. A monologue in iambic pentameter is particularly useful.

Whatever speech is chosen, it needs to be written down, printed out or photocopied, as students will need to mark the end of each sentence with //. Ask them to breathe in. Now use the breath (all of it) to chant the sentence, all on one note. Breathe in again. Now chant the next sentence. And so on. They should not worry, for now, about having to pause at the end of each sentence while the in-breath is taken. Repeat the exercise, but this time the speech should be spoken not chanted.

Next, ask students to mark the speech they are using with a /wherever there is a comma, a colon or semicolon. These are places to take a 'catch breath' so that they pause as briefly as possible before beginning the next phrase.

Students should notice that if they breathe correctly – that is, at the end of each sentence (//) or phrase (/) – it not only helps you speak but also makes sense of the speech because they are using the breath to support the punctuation of the piece. It also means that breathing is corresponding to the thought-patterns of the character.

Can you understand what they are saying?

In life, most of us do not articulate clearly. We swallow some of our words. We don't sound the ends of them properly. We can get away with this in one-to-one conversation but, if this happens when performing, the audience will find it hard to understand what the character is saying. You probably think this is a statement of the obvious. So do I. Yet, as an examiner, I have seen far too much work where my one chance to grasp what a character is saying is lost because inadequate attention has been paid to the importance of articulation. Performers and their teacher or director become overfamiliar with the material. We must always bear in mind that an audience has a single opportunity to understand what is being communicated.

Exercise 2: Articulation

The main muscles that support vocal clarity are the tongue, the cheeks and the lips. These muscles need to be warmed up and exercised.

If your students are unused to such work, it is worth flagging up that they will feel like ten types of idiot at first. Such feelings of self-consciousness are understandable but must be worked through, not used as an excuse to abandon the exercise.

1. Ask students to massage their own face all over with their hands.

Next, they should screw up the face very small and tight as if sucking a lemon. Then make the face as wide as possible. If a visual image is required, try a cartoon of surprise and shock: everything gaping and wide, wide, wide. Repeat this five times.

Next, pout then blow through the lips. They will find the sound that comes out is something like a donkey or a small motorbike.

Next, repeat the following tongue-twisters several times, as fast as possible, exaggerating the lip movements and sounding all the ends of words clearly.

- Particularly the tip of the tongue, the lips and the teeth.
- Betty bought a bit of butter.
- Red lorry yellow lorry.
- Unique New York.
- She sells seashells on the seashore. The shells she sells are seashells I'm sure.
- I swapped my Irish wristwatch for a Swiss wristwatch.

2. Next, ask the students to stand as for Exercise 1, above. They should take particular care that they are looking directly ahead and that the head is not tilted up or down, and that the neck is not leaning to one side. Ask them to visualise a dartboard on the opposite side of the room. The idea is that they will aim and throw the following sounds at the dartboard.

T–T–T   D–D–D

C–C–C   G–G–G

P–P–P   B–B–B

They should articulate the sound rather than the letter, e.g. 'tuh' not 'tee', etc. Build up the sequence gradually. First, one at a time, then in pairs, then the entire sequence.

3. Ask a student to find a piece of text to read aloud, slowly. I don't like Gilbert and Sullivan myself but many of the former's lyrics are particularly useful for this, especially 'The Modern Major General.'

- Read the text aloud, slowly, making sure lip movements are exaggerated and the end of each word is sounded clearly. Read it again, faster, but still making sure the words are sounded clearly. Remind students to breathe properly (as in Exercise 1) as well.

Exercise 3: Vocal Clarity

Clarity depends on articulation but also on whereabouts in the mouth the sound is produced. Most people speak from the back of the mouth. To attain vocal clarity, you need to help students bring their voice forward in the mouth. The following exercise is the single most useful thing I know to do this. It is also the exercise I have used most often when I visit and work with students on their devised work in progress.

1. Ask students to choose a line that they speak in their play. It should be around ten words. (If their dialogue is not yet fixed, assign them a tongue-twister or a line from the text used in Exercise 2). Ask them to let the mouth hang open and to let the tongue hang out over the lower lip. Breathe, then speak the line. It will come out as a series of incoherent sounds but they should attempt to make it as clear as possible (although they are doomed to fail). This involves the cheek muscles in the process.

2. Immediately, ask them to speak the line in the normal way. They should be able to hear (and indeed feel) that the sound is both clearer and further forward in the mouth.

The more indistinct their speech is, the more they need to apply this technique. If necessary, get them to run an entire scene in this way, or the entire play. (It also helps to get them to watch singers, particularly those from the gospel tradition, use their cheek muscles to shape and project sound – indeed, any of your students who also sing can make that connection with a nudge in that direction).

Exercise 4: Volume

A pairs exercise, to try when lines are more or less fixed. The pair should sit opposite, knees touching, speaking the lines softly and holding eye contact.

1. Ask the same pair to remain sitting opposite each other but as far apart as your working space will allow. They must rerun the scene, with the same intensity and intentions, but audible to each other. The others in the group have permission to call out 'Can't hear you!' when they can't.

2. Next, seat the pair a couple of metres apart, facing the audience. The same principle regarding interruption applies.

A couple of overall points before moving from the technical to the interpretative aspects of characterisation.

- Watch out for an 'energy drop' at the end of lines. This may be because there is inadequate breath to support the entire line.

- Watch out for students imposing a rising inflexion at the end of a line. In general, a full stop requires a falling inflexion.

- Even when a student is articulating clearly, if dialogue involves a word finishing in a 't' or a 'd' followed by a word that begins with a 't' or a 'd', then you need to ensure they sound both separately, rather than elide them.

2. Characterisation

Sometimes, candidates get high marks for playing characters close to their own personality. This can be wildly irritating, especially if the student is a powerful enough presence in their group to twist the narrative in that direction. However, it's legitimate for them to depict a version of themself. The examiner doesn't know what they're actually like. Indeed, many successful actors specialise in playing slight variations of themselves, or at least the persona they have constructed. Some actors (student or otherwise) are more comfortable with low- or high-status roles. Some are more convincing playing working class than middle class, or vice versa. As the student resource sheets suggest, your candidates need to understand their strengths and weaknesses to access high attainment. Often though, versatility is required, given that most devised work involves playing several roles.

Regardless of which character or characters are student is playing, the key question when watching work in progress is simply:

Is the student convincing in the role?

If the answer is 'no', what specifically is lacking? The following questions, and the exercises and tips that follow each one, will help address the issue, whatever that issue might be.

I begin with practical, kinaesthetic approaches to character because, in the same way as in Structure 5: No Inspiration Required, the simple act of moving can stir the imagination. However, these approaches should not be seen as contradictory or incompatible with the more psychologically based approach derived from Stanislavsky and outlined on student resource sheet 3: Developing a Character in Depth and Detail. It is important to stress that my starting point may not be your starting point. There are several routes through the process of developing an authentic, convincing character appropriate to the style and form of a piece of theatre. The more strategies you use for creating depth and detail in characterisation, the higher the attainment will be.

Does the student move in a way that is appropriate to the character, in general or at a particular moment?

Most students understand, well before they begin exam preparation, that body language is an important way of communicating what a particular character is like. A theoretical understanding does not necessarily translate into practical application! This first sequence can be assigned at the start of Stage 2, when students are first beginning to make decisions about characterisation. Or it can be used in Stage 3, if those decisions need to be consolidated or modified – or if the need to make such decisions appears to have slipped a student's mind. It also works as a whole-group starter exercise, or a series of starter exercises, at the appropriate point in the process.

Exercise 5: Physical Approaches to Characterisation

Explain the purpose of the work to the group: different people move in different ways and, when walking, 'lead' from different parts of the body. An actor needs to know which part of the body they lead from. To determine this, first ask the students walk as normally as possible around the studio. Next, the student should adapt their own movement by imagining that there is a string pulling from the head, then the chest, then the hips, then the knees. Finally, they should try walking as if the legs are heavy, then as if the feet are light. Discuss what sort of characters and situations each different way of moving suggests. Ask half the group to observe, then swap in order that each student gets feedback on:

- Where they lead from, which may or may not be appropriate for the character(s) being played.
- A range of other possibilities for characterisation, depending on the types suggested by leading from other parts of the body.

Next, ask students to work in pairs so they can observe and advise each other. (If the focus is on a particular scene, and one of the group does not appear in that scene, they can take on the role of monitor/director.) They should take it in turns to move as if:

- It is a freezing cold day.
- It is a hot and sweaty day.

- They were a very old person.
- They are trying to sneak in late at night without being heard or discovered.

Feedback to the performer should take the form of three specific points about what has altered, for example: do they walk faster or slower? Is the body tense or relaxed? Do they look straight ahead, from side to side, or down? Also – to open up possibilities and parallels – what other situation or person does that way of moving suggest? There is no right or wrong answer. The point is to identify what makes that state, and the movement that results from that state, different from the partner's normal movement and useful in making character choices.

As you know, there are other physical ways into character. You can assign animal characteristics. You can assign the Seven Deadly Sins. You can use the Laban technique. All of these are particularly useful if the style of physicalisation is heightened or stylised at any point in the play.

Does the student use a vocabulary appropriate to the character?

Anything that jolts an audience – and particularly a visiting examiner – out of the reality of the piece they are watching is bad news. There is nothing that does this as quickly and effectively as inappropriate use of language. I don't mean profanity: this may or may not be appropriate, depending on the character and situation (and your own ground rules about what language is not permissible). I mean the use of words and phrases that clearly come from the mouth of the candidate not the character. It is a telltale indication of a basic lack of attention to detail, which is likely to be borne out in other aspects of that performance and in the overall piece.

Of course, this is a further indication of the need for research, both factual (into the period and social milieu in which the piece is set) and imaginative (into the character being portrayed). However, we all have access to more vocabularies than we realise. It's easier to access these spontaneously. So I recommend that the following exercise is teacher-led and done as a whole-class exercise, early in Stage 2 of the process.

Exercise 6: Vocabularies

Ask students to find a partner. It does not have to be someone in their performance group. Next, they should decide who is A and who is B. Give them the first of the following scenarios and ask them to spontaneously improvise. Stop them after thirty seconds or so. Ask them to find another partner. Assign a different scenario. Let them improvise for the same length of time or thereabouts. Keep adding different pairs and different scenarios. Also, return to previous scenarios, in a random sequence: the pair involved should pick up that scenario at the point that they were stopped previously. Pace is important, in order that students find themselves using appropriate language, rather than make conscious decisions about appropriate language.

You can vary the scenarios as you think best. However, the aim is that they create a range of different ways of using language such as:

- Teenagers talking slang.
- Old people comparing symptoms and ailments and/or discussing their grandchildren.
- A formal interview.
- A dodgy mechanic and a customer who knows nothing about cars.

Discuss how this activity accessed the different vocabularies, rhythms and tones that we all absorb without being aware that we are doing so. Facilitate specific examples of those differences.

The exercise can also be done as a spontaneous solo improvisation. In which case, freeze the students between each character, then ask them to move to a different part of the room. For solo work in a range of vocabularies and tones, try:

- A sports commentator.
- An MP making a speech.
- A tour guide.
- A wildlife documentary commentary.
- Accepting an Oscar for Best Actor.
- A headteacher reprimanding a group of students for letting the school down.

Vocabulary is only one aspect of character. It is worth asking students to identify how their body language changed according to the character and situation they were improvising, to reinforce the connection between speech and stance.

Exercise 7: 'How (Not) To . . . '

This exercise focuses students' attention on appropriate speech in different contexts. It is useful if they don't seem to have grasped social codes and appropriate behaviour in the world they have created.

Ask the group to prepare and then show a scene using the techniques employed by adverts and/or training videos on 'How To . . . ' ('Get On at School', 'Do Well at a Job Interview', 'Meet the Future In-Laws' – or whatever takes their fancy).

They should produce two versions. The official version and a satirical version that, in real life, would ensure that the viewer failed abysmally to impress teachers, an interviewer, the in-laws-to-be. If time is a concern, they need only produce 'How (Not) To . . . '

Once the scenes have been shown, ask them to deconstruct what they have shown and decide how it might apply to their work in progress. You will note that the criterion imposed encourages the use of non-naturalistic techniques such as direct address.

Does the student know why they are speaking?

As an examiner, I often see a performer who appears to know *how* a character speaks – not the accent or the dialect, but the tone of voice, and whether this is sad or angry or deliriously happy. What is often missing is a sense of *why* a character speaks, that is, what they want to communicate to the other character(s) or to the audience. The following exercises help a student to clarify their intentions and objectives for, if they are not clear, how will the audience understand?

You could argue that this has as much to do with communication as it does with characterisation. I include it here because the context is an individual actor being clear on what they want. That clarity, or lack of it, affects clarity of intonation, inflexion and emphasis. However, both exercises can also be applied to ensure that a specific scene is working. The first one also works well as a whole-group starter activity.

Exercise 8: What's My Objective?

A needs to persuade B to do or give them something. If it makes life easier, assign what that is. Perhaps they want to borrow money or an item of clothing. Perhaps they want to persuade a friend to lie on their behalf. Regardless, they should spontaneously improvise the scene.

Now, ask the students to deconstruct the interaction. Regardless of the tactics A employed, and whether or not they succeeded in getting what they wanted, A's objective is clear: to persuade. The question to ask is what was B's objective? It could be a range of things, depending on how they dealt with the request. It can be easier for an observer to identify the objective than it is for the performer, hence the question should be addressed to the audience as well as the actors.

I often ask actors to 'raise the stakes', to make getting what the character wants, or preventing what they don't want, more vitally important.

Exercise 9: What's My Intention?

Ask the student to select one of the following lines:

- 'I've got some news!'
- 'Give me the money.'

Choose an emotion that they think fits the line. They should experiment, saying it as if they are:

- Very angry.
- Very excited.
- Very miserable.
- Very nervous.

That's *how* the line might be spoken but the point is to be aware of *why* it is said this way. To do this, ask the student to invent a character to say the line and the situation in which they might say it. For instance, the first line might be a friend who wants *to boast* that she has won the lottery or a child who wants *to break the news* that she has been in big trouble at school. The second line might be spoken by a beggar who needs *to ask for help* because they have no money for food; alternatively, it might be spoken by someone who is holding up a bank and wants *to threaten* a cashier.

If you or your students want to do more detailed work in this area, I recommend *Actions: The Actor's Thesaurus* by Marina Calderone and Maggie Lloyd-Williams.

Does the characterisation lack depth and detail?

If the answer to this question is 'yes', then it needs to be deconstructed in the same way that the question we began with – Is the actor convincing in the role? – has been, throughout this section.

It may be that the lack of depth and detail is related to one of the areas of characterisation already discussed – movement, language, clarity of intentions and so on. If it is due to none of these things, then the question to ask is this:

Has the student considered the character's backstory?

A character brings their history with them, just as we all do in real life. Not just what has happened a long time ago but what has happened immediately before. So the actor needs to know a character's backstory. The Stanislavsky questions listed on student resource sheet 3 (page 149) will help with this.

This seems the appropriate place to discuss hot-seating, which is often used as an explorative strategy or as a means of developing depth and detail. It can be useful, in the right context. This might be when exploring and developing a character, or the rest of the group could ask the Stanislavsky questions, once the character begins to take shape.

However, hot-seating is actively unhelpful if the questions are to do with facts as opposed to what is imagined. What was your role in the Battle of Trafalgar? What was it like growing up Black in the Deep South in 1953? How would they know? There is no substitute for factual, historical research, which can then be developed by using Exercise 11 (page 171) to establish a connection with the character's experience.

The following exercise is not only for establishing what has happened immediately before a character makes her or his entrance, but also a useful exercise in Stage 3, to help structure or shape a scene which may well begin sooner or later than it should, for maximum effect.

Exercise 10: 'Before the Scene Started, I . . . '

Ask the student to enact what is happening immediately before their entrance into a scene. This should include any interaction with other characters, whether or not we see those characters in the piece. They should go straight into the scene. Next time they run the scene, the chances are that the memory of what has happened immediately before will improve their performance.

Is the student commenting on the character?

By and large, actors want love and approval. Your students are no exception. After all, the extent of the examiner's approval is expressed by the mark they award, so approval equals attainment! Although some people enjoy the release of playing villains, this desire for love and approval can lead to an inability to get inside an unsympathetic character. Enabling students to discover and use what they have in common with a character will improve their performance. Finding a personal source will enable them to make the imaginative leap from their own experience into the character's experience. It is useful to stress that, if playing a murderer, a child abuser or a violent alcoholic, the character will be saying and doing things that the actor would not dream of doing, and that a reluctance to go there is understandable. As Dominic West said of his BAFTA-winning performance as the child-abusing mass-murderer and rapist, Fred West, 'This is very, very dangerous territory, but necessarily one has [to find] something in common.' However, finding a connection is vital, irrespective of who the character is, if an actor is to stand in a character's shoes and see things from the character's vantage point. Johnny Galecki, who plays Leonard in *The Big Bang Theory,* put it nicely when discussing the cast's preparation to play a group of near-genius scientists with autistic tendencies: 'We did try. We talked to physicists at UCLA. We watched *Nova.* I tried to read some books but they gave me anxiety attacks by page two. We realised that we can't pretend to think like geniuses. But we can learn to relate to them emotionally.'

The following two exercises – one solo, one in pairs, both based on Stanislavsky's sense-memory exercises – facilitate the empathy required to relate emotionally to the character. Both exercises are more useful in the latter part of Stage 2 or in Stage 3 of the devising process as they require characters and scenes to be fairly fixed.

Of course, certain performance styles require that the actor comments on the character but that, being a conscious choice, is different from the problem identified here.

Exercise 11: A Personal Source

Ask the student to list and record what they know about the character and the situation the character is in. They should not overlook the obvious, such as gender and age. (This is also useful as a way of monitoring if they are being as specific as necessary. Everyone knows how old they are so it's a worrying indication if you are told that a character is 'about fourteen'!)

Next, ask them to describe what the character feels about the situation they are in. This might be that the character:

- Has lost something or someone very important to them ('loss' does not have to mean death).
- Is experiencing hostility.
- Feels no one understands their situation.
- Feels frustrated and powerless.

Next, ask the student to write a paragraph describing a situation they have experienced that connects with the character whose speech you have chosen. This should be written in the present tense – 'I am sitting in my bedroom' – not 'I was sitting in my bedroom'. The focus should be on what could be seen, heard, smelled, touched and tasted rather than on the emotion experienced.

If the student has a particularly personal or painful experience in mind, they should think about whether they want to remember it, or use it in this activity. They should also think about whether they would feel comfortable telling others about it, or allowing them to read it. If the answer is 'No' then, another experience should be chosen.

Finally, ask the student to read the paragraph aloud. Prime the student and the others involved that they should then go straight into the scene that is causing problems.

Exercise 12: Storytelling

In pairs: A tells B a story about a time A felt grown up.

It should be a story that A feels comfortable sharing with B and, eventually, with the rest of the group. It does not need to be a 'big event' story.

A should focus on the senses (what they could see, hear, feel, taste or smell), not on the emotions they experienced. B's task is to listen actively and supportively, also to question, to clarify and ensure detail and to ensure that A focuses on senses. Then reverse.

Create an audience with a storyteller's chair. Each must tell their partner's story, in the first person (which is to say 'I' not 'she' or 'he'), to the rest of the group.

Apart from facilitating empathy, this exercise also develops the ability to listen and respond, as well as affirming that a student's experience has meaning and worth, and that an audience can be engaged by a story simply and truthfully told.

Are the different characters being played actually different from each other?

Playing multiple roles is not a problem in and of itself. It can enable candidates to score marks for their versatility and range. The drawback is that they need to demonstrate a degree of versatility and range.

All the previous exercises regarding all aspects of characterisation can and should be applied to each and every character that a student plays, even if that character only appears in a single scene and utters a single line (or no lines at all).

The following exercises also help ensure instant differentiation of the various characters played by a single actor. Indeed, they also support a clear distinction between the range of emotional states portrayed by a single character, at different points in the action.

Exercise 13: Transformation

Within the group, list the different characters that each student is playing. Next, they should create a solo frozen picture, showing how that character typically stands or sits and with a typical gesture incorporated. Ask the students to help each other to make the physicalisations as bold and exaggerated as possible: they can always be pulled back in, if necessary. The purpose, at this point, is to establish what makes them different from each other.

Number each image. Ask one student to lead the transformation, first to a count of ten, then to a count of five, then from one to the other on the snap of the fingers or the clap of a hand. They should take as long as the count or clap to complete the transformation, so that it moves slowly, at a medium pace or instantly. To begin with, they should go through the images in numerical order. Then assign one of the group to shout out numbers at random, so that they transform back and forward.

Although the exercise is designed to be applied to established character, it can also be used earlier in the devising process, if the piece involves exaggerated characterisation or characters based on stereotypes. In which case, ask each member of the group to pick four stereotypes to embody in the same way.

Exercise 14: Triggering

A useful exercise in Stage 3, for hitting the ground running when a student is playing several characters and/or the narrative moves backwards and forwards in time.

Ask each student to come up with a trigger. This might be expressed as an image or colour or phrase or metaphor or piece of music. There is no right or wrong answer: whatever works for them as stimulus to find and express the character's state at the start of that scene. They should then go through every entrance in the piece, preceding each entrance with a statement about what their trigger is. If it doesn't seem to help, then they are using the wrong trigger and should find a different one.

Is the student gesturing too much? Or gesturing inappropriately?

There's an awful lot of arm-waving on stage. It's not confined to devised student drama and it's clearly been the case for centuries, given that Shakespeare, using Hamlet as his mouthpiece, told the Player King: 'Do not saw the air too much'.

It is odd but true that arm-waving seems to dissipate a performer's vocal energy. It is as if the energy flies out of their fingertips and splatters in all directions, rather than being focused in the appropriate direction.

Over-gesticulation usually stems from the same source as the meandering around stage identified later in this section. If, in Stage 3, you feel that sawing the air is a problem for a particular student, simply ask them to do the speech sitting on their hands or, if they are in motion, with another member of the group holding their hands by their sides, by hugging them (gently!) from behind.

That's remedial work, as it were. To avoid such intervention, students should be encouraged to discover the character's gestural vocabulary earlier in the process, at the same time as they are exploring how the character moves, sits and stands.

Exercise 15: Appropriated Gesture

Ask students to work in pairs. They should sit opposite each other and watch how the other gestures in conversation. They may know that anyway. Student A should mimic student B's gestures and way of sitting, then vice versa. (It's as well to forewarn them that this exercise can make a person extremely self-conscious!)

Next, ask them to mimic the gestures of people they know. If this flummoxes them, ask them to do some people-watching before the next rehearsal session. However, most students can mimic their teachers' gestures, including yours, with depressing accuracy. That makes a good starting point. They do not both need to know the person whose gestures are being replicated but they should both experiment with every set of gestures offered, to open up possibilities. Self-awareness is the key: a character may have some of the actor's characteristics but that, ideally, is by choice rather than her or his default position.

Exercise 16: Magnifying the Gesture

This exercise is helpful for chorus work and for pieces or sequences where the style is large and bold so the action needs to be magnified or heightened.

Ask everyone in the group to sit as still as possible, in a circle. There will be small shifts and movements. If anyone notices any movement, mannerism, gesture from another member of the group, they should imitate but magnify the movement. So a slight shrug becomes a massive one; a tap of a foot becomes a stamp and so on. Inevitably, a third person in the group will see the second person's magnified movement. That third person' task is to make the movement bigger still.

Is the student's face expressive enough?

Some people's faces are more mobile than others. This is fact. Some students are so expressionless that they appear to have been Botoxed. There are all sorts of reasons why a student's real life might cause them to try to mask their emotions. However, it's not what you want on stage.

Often, a lack of facial expression, like a lack of vocal expression, means that the student has not rooted himself or herself in the character or the situation. The exercises that follow, on intentions and objectives, should remedy this, if this is the cause of the problem. The overarticulation mentioned in the section on voice has the useful side effect of leading to exaggerated movement of the face. The following exercises should also help, too:

Exercise 17: The Beaufort Scale

Assign a range of contrasting emotions to the group. Ask them in turn to express one of these emotions – physically and facially – as a frozen image. The emotion might be anger or sorrow or fear – whatever is required. Ask the rest of the group to say where on a scale of one to ten they would place the image. One is barely perceptible, ten is stratospherically expressed. They should all replicate the image at the level they agree. Then take it in turns to call out numbers up or down the scale or both.

You will notice that this exercise is also good for creating a similar level of expressiveness within the group. The following exercise is useful for that, too, as well as being a fun way of connecting with various emotions and making them bigger.

Exercise 18: Pass the Emotion

Arrange the group, standing, in a circle. Explain that there is an imaginary ball (the size of a football rather than a tennis ball) that contains an emotion. Ask the group to decide on the emotion that the ball contains. Then one member of the group is assigned to cross the space, with the imaginary ball, to spread the emotion around. They should move in the manner of the word, so that the emotion is physicalised (including facial expression). How the person transports the ball (perhaps bouncing it, perhaps kicking it, perhaps carrying it) is up to them, as is how they pass the ball to the person on the other side of the circle. However, the moment the ball is passed, it transforms the received instantly into whatever the first person is representing and however they are representing it. Change the emotion, as required.

That student is just wandering around the stage! What do I do to stop this?

You'll note that the question refers to the student rather than the character. This is because it's usually the performer fidgeting rather than enacting character choices.

Admittedly, it is very hard to have the confidence to stand still and just be, on stage. Somehow, we feel that moving makes the scene or us more interesting. Too much motion, individually or collectively, may be to do with this. It may be connected with the staging and blocking of a scene, in which case the exercises listed under staging should help. It may be to do with lack of clarity regarding the purpose of a scene or sequence, in which case see the relevant exercises under communication.

Here are two quick exercises that can be applied to an individual:

Exercise 19: Sticky Feet

Ask the student to imagine that their feet stick to the stage, so every move requires far more effort than usual. If they lack imagination, weight the feet. No, really.

Exercise 20: Convalescence

Ask the actor to remember an occasion when they were exhausted, post-operative or just recovering from a heavy cold or other illness that rendered them bed-bound. Every movement is an effort. Perform the scene with that in mind.

If neither of these do the trick, then simply stop the scene every time they move unnecessarily and ask the student to justify the move. If they can't, then they shouldn't. Or assign someone in the group to monitor in this brutal yet effective way.

3. Visibility

Is there an awareness of the importance of how the piece is staged?

I address visibility before communication for the same reason that I addressed audibility at the start of the section on characterisation. Without it, you're in trouble. We're back to the nightmare vision outlined in the introduction to this book, where students have no sense of how to stage their piece.

Undoubtedly much of what underpins a group's awareness of where they are on stage and why emerges through their creative choices. However, these three technical exercises foreground the importance of proxemics and staging, particularly for those who lack spatial awareness.

Exercise 21: House on a Mountain Top

This is a useful whole-group starter activity to try early in Stage 2 of the devising process. The exercise can be repeated, without the elements of surprise and guesswork, to consolidate awareness of spatial relationships.

Mark out a large square. A volunteer – whom we shall call V – leaves the room. Four or five volunteers offer to play the family. V is the fiancé(e) of one family member. The family has a secret: their house is balanced on the pinnacle of a very high mountain. Everyone needs to be counterbalancing each other at all times, otherwise the house will fall off the top of the mountain, slide down and everyone will die. (I accept that this exercise requires a hefty suspension of disbelief.)

V enters the scene, having been told there is a secret that they must guess. Where V moves will determine how the family have to adjust their positions – and how they rationalise those adjustments, to avoid revealing the secret to V. The audience is allowed to freeze the action to adjust positioning of family members, without revealing why. The exercise continues until V has guessed or given up.

Exercise 22: Don't Enter the Triangle!

An exercise that is particularly good for groups who always end up standing too close together, obscuring each other from the audience. Actually, although I call it 'an exercise', it's more of an ongoing aspect of their devising process, until their sight-line problems are solved or, at least, an awareness of importance of sight lines developed.

Mark out their performing area, then mark a triangle (or curve) with the apex at the centre of the stage and the two points extreme downstage-left and extreme downstage-right. Forbid the cast to stand in the triangle, if there are more than two people on stage. Not necessarily forever but until they stop clumping together, blocking our view of the action.

Exercise 23: Playing the Cross

Mark out a cross on the performing area. One line of it should run from downstage-left to upstage-right. The other, it follows, will run from downstage-right to upstage-left. The point at which the lines cross will be centre stage.

This is useful in various ways:

- It encourages students to play scenes on diagonals, rather than opposite each other in line with the front of the stage.
- It gives guidance for the best way to arrange group scenes so that sight lines are maintained and one character is not blocking another.
- It makes visible the fact that the centre stage is the focal point for the audience's attention.

A few general points about staging, before moving onto the various aspects of communication:

- Even skilled and experienced performers are disadvantaged and discombobulated by stepping in front of an audience only to discover that the performance area is wider or deeper or less so than what they've been used to. For this reason, I always have a mark-up on the rehearsal-room floor, delineating the size of the stage. I realise this is easier in a designated rehearsal space than in a drama studio, assuming that you teach in a studio and not a classroom. However, if you have sufficient space, it's very useful to mark out the size of the performance area, at least somewhere in the studio – rotate where groups rehearse so each has access to it. Or mark out the corners with chairs.

- The vast majority of the devised work I have seen is staged end-on. The temptation to stipulate that pieces must be staged in this way is powerful given that this is the easiest configuration to film and that most exam boards require a filmed record of the piece. However, how a piece is staged is connected to use of form. So if a group can present a convincing case for traverse, theatre-in-the-round, promenade, thrust, whatever, then let them stage it in that way. You'll know how they want to stage it well before the performance examination date. There will be time to work out the logistics.

- Regardless of how the piece is configured and staged, don't seat the examiner too close to the action. They should be able to take in the whole stage, most of the time, without turning the head.

- Don't seat the examiner too far away either! There may be volume issues. Also, too great a space between audience and performance unwittingly conveys a lack of confidence. Monitor the group in rehearsal: if they routinely avoid using the front of the stage, they will convey a sense of a group who are literally retreating before they have even begun.

- Split focus may be a useful strategy for process work. It rarely succeeds in performance. Far too often, I've sat there, staring at an empty space in the centre of the stage, wondering why I'm constantly looking from left to right and back again, in the manner of a spectator at Wimbledon's Centre Court. I would argue that this to-ing and fro-ing isn't really split focus at all, it's more alternating focus. If a group wants to intercut scenes, it is far better for them to establish a convention for having the scenes taking place in the same place, but freezing the action of one while the other talks through and moves as if the characters in the other are not there. Which, in the reality of the respective scenes, they are not. Or to find a movement convention for rotating and revolving the action. (The exercises on transitions, entrances and exits later in this section will also help with this.)

- It is a fallacy that a performer should never have their back to the audience. So long as it is intentional, and so long as the effect has been considered, why not?

4. Communication

There are two key concepts that underpin how effectively a performance communicates its intentions to an audience.

The first is *narrative economy*. Far too often, a piece or scene is cluttered with extraneous material, be that movement, dialogue, a scene or a sequence that overstays its welcome.

The second is *clarity*. Clarity with regard to what effect they want to achieve and how they are demonstrating their understanding of the ways in which theatre can communicate to achieve it. All the activities in this section are designed to ensure that, so far as is possible, both narrative economy and clarity are realised in performance.

First, though, three exercises to ensure that the ensemble communicate with each other. While 'ensemble' may suggest a particular style and form of piece to you, I use the word in preference to 'cast', as previously mentioned. An ensemble is defined as 'a group of musicians, actors, or dancers who perform together' or 'a unit or group of complementary parts that contribute to a single effect'. Surely both of those express our aspiration and aims for how our students should work together and what we hope they will achieve, regardless of the style, content and form of their piece?

Is the ensemble energised?

It is always dispiriting to see a group shuffle into a studio: we know that performance requires a basic level of energy. So does rehearsing. Both the following exercises are highly effective as part of a whole-class warm-up, too. Once you have demonstrated them with and to the whole group, in the way described below, they can use them within their individual performance groups. Both are invaluable to hurl in for two minutes if a group or the whole class's energy or focus is flagging, regardless of which stage of the devising/rehearsal process you are at.

Exercise 24: Energy Clap

The group stand in a circle, large enough that everyone can make eye contact with everyone else without having to step back.

The teacher makes eye contact with anyone in the circle (more or less opposite at the start) and throws the energy clap to that person. This is done by clapping and, as you do so, extending the hands until the arms are straight in the direction of the person with whom eye contact is made. That person (the catcher) receives the energy clap by reversing the gesture, e.g. palms together with arms outstretched to receive, then pull arms back and separate hands as they land against the sternum.

Immediately the catcher becomes the thrower and makes eye contact with anyone else in the circle and the movements are repeated. The aim is to keep the same rhythm, rather than try to catch each other out.

You need to ensure that everyone follows the invisible energy being clapped across the circle with their eyes – not least because this mean everyone will be looking at the catcher who will then be able to throw to anyone without pausing for thought.

The arm movements should be committed – that is to say, fully extended – and the claps vigorous: if the palms don't sting slightly by the end, it's not working.

Once the method and rhythm are established, speed up the pace. Then start varying the trajectory of the energy clap. Then start moving, at the same speed, in the same direction around the circle, while playing the game. Then break so as everyone is moving freely around the room, but maintaining eye contact with as many other people as possible.

Exercise 25: Cherry Picking

Ask the group to stand in a circle, far enough apart to ensure that they have sufficient space to swing their arms without clouting the person next to them. As with vocal warm-ups, feet should be parallel to legs, legs should be in line with the hips and knees should be unlocked.

Repeat the following sequence four times. The pace should be fast but not frenetic. Everyone, at the start of the appropriate movement, should speak the number of each move, loudly and clearly. They should remember to breathe in before each number. Each time the sequence is repeated, the stretch should be slightly further extended.

1. Reaching up, extend the right hand across the body to the left side.
2. Reaching up, extend the left hand across the body to the right side.
3. In a line with the shoulder, extend the right hand across the body to the left side.
4. In a line with the shoulder, extend the left hand across the body to the right side.
5. Leaning down, extend the right hand across the body to the left side.
6. Leaning down, extend the left hand across the body to the right side.
7. Leaning further down (so the tips of the fingers touch the floor if possible) extend the right hand across the body to the left side.
8. Leaning further down (so the tips of the fingers touch the floor if possible) extend the left hand across the body to the right side.

Next, repeat the sequence four times. Instead of the number, the in-breath should be exhaled through the teeth (so the teeth need to be together, but not gritted.) This will produce a 'sssssh' sound.

Is the ensemble focused on and attuned to each other?

I don't have to tell you how important this is, both in rehearsal and in performance.

I start every rehearsal process with the following exercise, whether devising with young people or rehearsing an existing script with professional actors. Apart from being great for group focus, it's extremely useful for establishing non-verbal communication, spatial awareness and relationships. Also, if you use it while you're still deciding performance groups, it's a handy way of observing who cooperates, who negotiates, who attempts to impose and to lead, and so on.

Exercise 26: Attuning

Ask everyone to walk neutrally, then freeze. Once these simple instructions have been understood, explain that their collective task is for everyone to walk and to freeze at the same time, without verbal cues or obvious physical ones, from the teacher or each other.

Once that has been established, introduce a new rule: only one person moves at any time, but as soon as they finish, another person – and only one person – starts moving and so on. Once the principle has been established, introduce the variation principle. Whoever moves must vary the length, rhythm, height and style of walk from what has gone immediately before. Counsel them not to think too much about what they're going to do. Just let it happen. Continue until they're moving as freely and unselfconsciously as possible.

Next, two people move at the same time, then three, then four. Round off the activity with a return to the whole group walking and freezing at the same time. It is useful to deconstruct the activity, to facilitate understanding of what skills were required for the exercise to succeed: observation, listening, use of peripheral vision, spatial awareness – and something which cannot be defined more precisely than 'allowing it to happen'.

Having looked at ways of establishing communication within the ensemble, we move to communication with the audience. The sequence of exercises begins with monologues, then moves to scenes, and then moves to consideration of the whole piece.

To return our earlier point about the arbitrary division of aspects of theatre for assessment purposes, you might ask why at least some of these activities are not included in the section on characterisation. They could well be: some can be used to help develop your students' understanding of characterisation. However, they are here because, primarily, they are concerned with the relationship between performer and audience.

Why is that direct address not working?

Whether it's a monologue or a piece of narration, a student needs to make decisions about three things if they are to communicate effectively with the audience:

- The imagined listener (an individual or group).
- Intention (*why* does a person speak?).
- Relationship to location (familiar/unfamiliar).

Exercise 27: The Imagined Listener

If you ask a student, rehearsing their monologue or direct address, to whom they are talking, the answer is likely to be either 'myself' or 'the audience'. Both may be true; neither is helpful. Talking to yourself leads to a lack of energy and ignores the fact that communication generally involves another person or people. Talking to the actual audience lacks the necessary precision and imagination to raise attainment.

This exercise works well as a whole-group starter: I would throw it in as part of Stage 1 of the devising process, particularly if the activities in that stage involve creating monologues. Or it can be given to an individual student – or a group of them – whose direct address is underwhelming.

First, tell the students that they have one line. That line is 'I've got something to tell you.' They must speak the line twice. Once to a single person and once to a group. It helps if they imagine a context. Perhaps they are a delighted child about to break the news of their exam results to a parent. Or maybe they are a primary-school teacher, about to break the news that the class guinea pig has died over the weekend. They should speak the line aloud. Ask the rest of the class (or the group, depending on when and how you are using the exercise) to identify which rendition is addressed to an individual and which to a group. Nine times out of ten they will do so successfully, because the tone of voice is different – and the body language probably is different, too.

Once this principle has been established, the student should experiment with their troublesome speech. Does the speech work best if every line is addressed to a group? Does it work best if every line is addressed to an individual? Does it work best if some lines are addressed to a group and some to an individual or to different individuals? But – and this is crucial – who do they picture that individual or group as being? In particular, what is the character's status in relation to the imagined listener? How does the character feel that what they have to say will be received? With approval or with disapproval? Are they picturing addressing an authority figure or are they confiding in a close friend? The latter is often appropriate given that most students understand that a soliloquy or a direct address is something that the character cannot say to the other characters on stage, for whatever reason.

Apart from trying the speech as if addressed to an authority figure and then to someone who can be confided in, assign some of the following (or substitute your own ideas), to see which works best. Regardless of the context and content of the actual speech, counterintuitive suggestions can lead to far greater clarity.

- Arrogantly and contemptuously, as if the audience are lucky to be in the presence of the speaker.
- As a stand-up comedian.
- As a politician, addressing a hostile audience.
- As if the audience are all much younger than the speaker.
- As if to a group of mates, first thing on Monday morning, gossiping about the weekend.

- As a seven-year-old needing reassurance from a parent.
- As if addressing an audience of old biddies, wanting to shock them.
- As if giving evidence in court.
- As if trying to remember something that happened a long, long time ago.

The imagined listener will determine the imagined location and the sense of the relationship to that place; in particular whether it is familiar or unfamiliar. This too will add depth and detail. Neither the imagined listener nor the imagined location need to have a direct connection to the play – they just need to open up possibilities: I refer you, and them, back to the Paul Hunter quote on page 57.

The next issue to address is *what* and *how much* is being said. As mentioned earlier, monologues often occur because it enables a character to say things they cannot say to other characters – certainly, that is the function of the soliloquy in the plays of Shakespeare and his contemporaries. The problem is often that stepping out of the action to address the audience also seems to involve stepping out of character. I think this stems from the use of the techniques of thoughts aloud and thought-tracking. These techniques tend to imply that what is revealed must be revealed through words when, in fact, focusing on other forms of communication will lead to more detailed, deep, interesting work. An understanding of subtext helps. This is discussed in answer to the question: 'Are they telling rather than showing?' The following exercise also helps. By focusing on an activity, it makes the delivery more believable and helps overcome the unnecessary emoting that limits marks.

Exercise 28: Distraction Through Action

The exercise works best when a speech is well developed, if not finally set. Have someone else in the group feed them the actor her or his lines if necessary. If they know the lines but start forgetting them, they should not panic. Even hardened professionals do the same when asked to do something new, as an experiment.

Try the speech as:

- A shy kid, fiddling with a security blanket, addressing two adults so the actor's eye line is upwards, as the imagined listener is taller.
- Collecting up items, addressing one person. You can scatter anything; the activity rather than objects is the point.
- While scratching an imaginary itch; make sure that the activity is established before the speech begins, to a group of people.
- While (miming) applying make-up, addressed to a single person; again, establish the activity before the speech begins.
- As if on stepping stones: jump, skip or step onto a new stone before each line.

Clarity regarding listener, location and how subtext is revealed should, as a bonus, stop the fidgeting and wandering around the stage that is the downfall of many a monologue. The vast majority of direct address works best if the speaker is sitting or standing, not wandering up and down the stage. It will also be enhanced by eye contact with the audience. This is daunting. (It doesn't need to be the examiner. In fact, I advise against button-holing her or him. They may be taking notes at that point anyway.) Eye contact can be faked. Find a fixed point immediately above the heads of the audience, at the back of the room. Problem solved.

Why is this scene not working?

As with the question, 'Is the actor convincing in the role?', if a scene or sequence is not working, then a series of subsequent questions are required. The first of these is:

Are the students telling rather than showing?

By telling, I mean that information is communicated explicitly, in speech. Devised drama can be overtalkative whereas, in real life, people's speech tends to evade, to avoid, to allude rather than to address directly. It might happen in a monologue, as suggested above, or in a scene, or it might infect the whole piece.

To ensure students understand the concept of narrative economy, I suggest the following two exercises are built into Stage 2 of the devising process, or (as per the answer to Question 3 in Part 1: Preparation) are part of your curriculum prior to beginning the devised work. Then revisit as and when required to modify a speech, a scene or a whole piece that tells us what should be revealed through action and interaction.

Exercise 29: Understanding Subtext

Ask students why someone might want to say something to someone but not feel able to do so. They should refer to their personal experiences. However, I always emphasise that no one should share any personal experience unless they feel comfortable doing so. The students will identify such reasons as because they are embarrassed, ashamed, worried, don't want to upset the listener or are fearful of the listener's reaction.

In pairs, ask each student to imagine that, on an empty chair, sits someone they don't want to say something to but have to approach. One should spontaneously improvise such a situation; the other should observe. Then reverse. Before the exercise, let them know that the observer's feedback to the performer should focus on how their reluctance to address the subject is made manifest, specifically:

- Their body language.
- Their eye contact, or lack of it, with the person on the chair.
- Their language, in particular the rhythm of it and whether and how they address what it is they have to say, or make excuses and end up talking about something else.

In the same pairs, read the following dialogue. They should not predetermine why A is apprehensive and B is angry, but they are, and the lines should be spoken with these moods in mind.

A. Are you all right?

B. Fine.

A. Is anything the matter?

B. No.

Show various versions and ask the audience what story emerges through playing this subtext. There will be different interpretations of the same dialogue and of the different versions of the same dialogue. This is the point, in order to establish:

- What is communicated subtextually.
- That sometimes people, in this case B, say the exact opposite of what they mean, and the more emphatic their denial, the less convinced we are that what they say is true.

Based on the above, elicit a definition of subtext from the group.

Exercise 30: Playing the Routine

This solo spontaneous exercise is a useful way to demonstrate how to communicate mood without saying, for instance: 'I'm really angry with you.'

Each student should pick a daily routine of their own. This routine – perhaps their morning ablutions or making a cup of tea – should be done as accurately as possible, without inflection. The aim is just to replicate it, miming props as necessary, so that what the routine is is clear to the audience. Having established the series and sequence of actions, ask students to do it again, but, this time, to add a mood or emotion. It works as a whole-class starter activity, or can be adapted and used within a group. They should not plan what impact this has on how they move through the sequence. They should just let it affect their actions.

Ask half the class to observe the other half perform their daily routines with the mood or emotion they have picked informing their actions. Discuss. Focus on specifics, not just: 'She used body language,' or 'He was in a bad mood,' but what precisely did they do or not do, with their face, focus, eye line or by using speed, pause, repetition that conveyed the mood? How did the mood affect and alter the overall rhythm and speed of the actions? Reverse, so the second half of the class perform while the first half watch and critique. A useful subsidiary learning point is that the actor's intention may communicate something other than what they intended. In some cases, these different interpretations are fine. In other cases, it may be that the performer is not doing enough or not doing what they are doing specifically enough.

If the use of subtext is clear and a scene is still not working, the next question to ask is:

What is going on in the scene and why?

The performers need to know why the scene is there (of which, more later). They need to be clear on the dynamics of the action and the inter-relationships of the characters. If they are not clear on these points, how can they hope to communicate clearly with the audience?

There are various exercises that can help clarify these points. This first is a general exercise, which also helps clarify the connection between intonation and intention. The next three are strategies to apply to a scene, once it is more or less set, to help provide the necessary clarity.

Exercise 31: The Yes/No Game

In pairs. One can only say 'Yes', the other can only say 'No'. The objective is to join partner on other side of room. So the way they say 'Yes', and the way the other responds, determines whether they move forward, stay static or move back.

Exercise 32: Game, Set and Match

Put a line down the middle of rehearsal studio. Play the scene like a tennis match. Every line should be accompanied by an appropriate action. The first line is the serve, the second is the return of serve, and so forth. The exercise works best for duologues, although can be adapted for doubles.

Exercise 33: Tug of War

Tie the performers together with rope so the scene becomes a two-, three- or four-way tug of war, exploring the tension and release within a passage of dialogue. It follows that there should be several metres of rope between them – this is not the three-legged race. It also follows that certain ground rules need to be imposed, particularly if one person in the scene is much physically stronger than the others.

Exercise 34: Web of Intimacy

Create a web for each character's perspective within the scene. The character is at the centre. They decide whom they feel most intimate with, and place that person at an appropriate distance. It follows that the character's antagonist is furthest out. (The configurations that come from this can be used as a starting image or transitional image, if appropriate.)

If this does not solve the problem, the question to ask is:

What is the point of this scene?

Does the scene convey a plot point? Does it let the audience know about a character or relationship? Does it communicate a mood? (Warning: not all actors are articulate. You know this already – doubtless, you've tried to squeeze evaluative comments out of some of them before now. So you may need to watch the scene – or ask another group to watch and say what they are getting from the scene – and whether or not that is the performers' intention.)

Following the same principle, it is useful to pair up two performance groups for the next exercise, to provide the necessary external perspective for each other.

Exercise 35: Distillation and Paring Down

The group should rehearse and show a silent version of the scene. It should not be a mime, but simply a scene where the body language, spatial relationships, the eye contact (or lack of it) and physical relationships create an atmosphere that captures what, for the group, is the essence of the scene. Show and discuss what has been communicated. Does it make sense?

The next step is to allow the reintroduction of a limited number of words. To begin with, allow precisely ten words – and that's between them, not each. How much of what needs to be communicated is missing? Far less than they imagine. They can put back in some words once you've made that point. This is useful in and of itself in supporting narrative economy, given the previously mentioned tendency for students to tell via dialogue what should be revealed through action.

In summary, then: agree (or uncover) the point and purpose of a scene, make that point or points, then move on! This should ensure that a scene finishes at an effective moment. On which point, the principle of beginning with a bang not a whimper applies to each scene as well as to the overall piece.

If there appears to be no point to a scene or if it appears to come, stylistically, from a different play, your options are simple. Cut it. Or rework it.

Does the scene lack tension?

Earlier, when discussing intentions and objectives (see Exercises 8 and 9 on pages 168–169), I mentioned the importance of an actor playing for high enough stakes. If a scene lacks tension, it may be that the student is not clear on what they want, or does not want it enough for the audience to care much, either way. The following exercises are useful in communicating the importance of building tension in a scene, or a whole piece. The first two exercises work best as whole-group starters; the final one can be assigned to an individual group at whatever stage in their process they need to be reminded of the importance of creating dramatic tension by building a sense of anticipation within a scene.

Exercise 36: The Emperor Game

This begins as Grandmother's Footsteps, the playground game. Assign a volunteer to stand at one end of the room, as the grandmother, facing away from the group. The rest of the group stand at the other end of the room, then try to sneak up on the grandmother. Whenever the volunteer turns, if the grandmother spots a person moving, however tiny the movement, the grandmother points at them, names them and they must return to their end of the room where they may begin their attempt to sneak up again. The game finishes when someone reaches the finishing line and touches the grandmother's shoulder. At which point they take over as the grandmother.

After a couple of rounds played in this way, vary the rules. In the next round, if someone is caught in motion, they are out and must sit at the side of the room until the round is completed.

In the next variation, the grandmother becomes the emperor. Explain to the class that the emperor has absolute power of life or death. Unfortunately for the rest of the group, the emperor is a capricious tyrant. When the emperor turns, if they see one of their subjects in motion, they name them and ask the question, 'Why are you sneaking up on your emperor?' Depending on the answer (which, obviously, must be improvised), the emperor pronounces sentence: 'Live!' or 'Die!' The former means that the subject remains in the game and can continue sneaking, when the emperor's back is once again turned. 'Die!' means that the subject must fall to the floor, where they remain sprawled until the end of the game. Protracted death agonies are to be encouraged – any physical response from one of the remaining, living subjects can be challenged by the emperor with their question. Make it clear to the group that, just because the answer, 'I am bringing you a lovely cake,' or 'I have come to warn you about a plot against your life,' works one time, there is no guarantee that it will persuade the emperor a second time.

This final round is likely to last far longer than the previous rounds, because the subjects have far more invested in it. They want to live! When it is finished, discuss how, even in a game, the dramatic tension was increased.

Exercise 37: 'Is There Anybody There?'

Explain that is a solo improvisation and that all the scenes will be created spontaneously and simultaneously. Ask each student to imagine that they are alone, in a room, at night. Each hears an unexpected and disconcerting noise. At what point in the scene they each hear that noise, and what type of noise it is, is up to the individual, as is the decision regarding whether the room is a familiar or unfamiliar place. The scene will last precisely one minute. There is a single line, which will occur at the end of the scene. That line is: 'Is there anybody there?' Announce every ten seconds what point they are at in the scene, then give them a countdown to the line in final five seconds. Everyone should speak the line simultaneously, in whatever tone seems appropriate.

Repeat immediately, half the class at a time, so that the students can develop and improve how they are communicating (without words), in their respective scenes, the rising tension and in order that those watching can observe and comment on how this is being done.

Exercise 38: Anticipation

Ask one person in the group to sit on a chair in a relaxed, comfortable manner. At a given signal, they should transform their posture and movement (or lack of it) to indicate that they are waiting for someone to arrive or for something to happen and that they are not looking forward to it. The group should take it in turns to be the person on the chair, and to find different ways to build up the atmosphere.

- What happens if the person keeps looking at her or his watch?
- What happens if they get up and pace from time to time?
- If they glance at the door?

Ask the students to discuss how these things create a tenser atmosphere and, crucially, how might they be incorporated into the scene in question?

Is a student overacting? Are they underacting?

The form of the piece will – or should – dictate the style of performance required. A piece that uses, say, *commedia dell'arte* or stereotypes necessitates a different style of performance to a piece using Brechtian conventions or a thoroughly naturalistic piece. So, consideration of whether the performance levels are consistent must always be seen within the context of what is required for the overall piece.

Underacting is often indicative of a lack of ownership. We all know the type of student who is happy to be told what to do and to say, and who does so to the best of their ability. Although exercises elsewhere should help galvanise this type of student, ultimately you may just have to live with a performer who lacks commitment or ability. (See Part 1: Preparation, Question 1 for the best ways of assigning groups in the first place). Overacting – or more precisely overreacting – often occurs because a student is overcompensating for what they feel their fellow performers should be providing but are not. Earlier exercises (try 17 and 18 on pages 176) will help raise the level of the others – if it actually needs to be raised. It may just be the perception of a committed, conscientious but overanxious candidate. A quiet word with the overcompensator helps too. They will understand that what is intended to be helpful will, in fact, create an imbalance within the scene and – this usually clinches the argument – have a negative effect on their mark.

Exercise 39: Fun Run

In which everyone plays someone else's part. Seeing your performance through someone else's eyes can help move you up or down the scale of over- or underacting. Be aware that this can be a chastening and upsetting experience. It needs to be a group who are secure with each other, else all your careful planning and assigning of groups may be undone. It also needs to be a group who are on top of the process, which may not be the case.

However, the real danger is the performer who just wants to emote all the time. You know the type: they begin over-the-top and work their way up from there. Watching someone sob or shout their way through a performance is almost guaranteed to make an audience stop listening within a couple of minutes. It also indicates that the overenthusiastic student in question has missed an essential point, which is this: it is always more interesting seeing someone trying not to cry than it is seeing someone cry. It is always more interesting seeing someone trying not to lose their temper than it is seeing someone rant and rave. Please, put that on a banner and hang it on your drama studio wall. Stamp it on the front of their folders. For me, the single most important thing you can teach your students is that suppression is better than release because a person trying to keep calm, to keep their emotions under control, is invariably more affecting than a person in floods of tears.

This is not to say that a character should never break down, or explode with anger. The point is the actor has to earn that release. Exercise 27 (pages 185–187) will help, as will the exercises that facilitate understanding of subtext (pages 189–191). However, the following will also help curb histrionic tendencies:

Exercise 40: How to Bank Emotion

Ask the student to conceive of the emotion, whether anger, despair or whatever, as an obstacle to communicating what they want. They should resist rather than succumb to it. To facilitate this, try some or all of the following. The student should perform the speech:

- As if giving evidence in court – they cannot allow themself to cry or to lose their temper. If they do, the other side will win the case. Every time emotion rises, the actor should breathe and pause for long enough to continue with it, suppressed.
- Trying to piece together the sequence of events, to remember in what order everything happened – this provides a helpful distance from the event and therefore from the emotion.
- Tapping foot. They should establish the rhythm before they begin their speech. No eye contact should be made with audience or fellow performers. Every time the emotion rises, breathe and pause for long enough to continue.

- Holding on to a chair, not moving on from each line until it has been pictured before being spoken.

In each and every one of these variations, the emotion may break through. That's fine, because the breakthrough is a genuine shift, rather than a default position. The scene or speech should be performed in this way to the rest of the group, or as part of a whole-class showing of work. This will confirm to the actor in question that banking the emotion is far more powerful, dramatically.

How are the group managing transitions and performance conventions?

In Part 1: Preparation, I pointed out that marks are available for how students move from scene to scene to another, because these are performance conventions and are thus related to their demonstration of their understanding of style and form. The following exercises are useful early in the process (or before you even begin the process) because they focus students on the need to build in such considerations from the beginning of the process rather than bolt them on at the end.

Exercise 41: From First Person to Third Person

I recommend this whole-group technical, teacher-led exercise as a means of showing students how to:

- Establish and explore the principle or convention of performers transforming from one character to another.
- Use storytelling and direct address in combination with dialogue.

You will need a script that involves direct address, where the actor moves from speaking about the character in the third person to becoming the character and speaking in the first person. I suggest either the opening of Neil Bartlett's adaptation of *Oliver Twist* (2004) or an extract from Tim Supple and Carol Ann Duffy's versions of *Grimm's Tales* (1993). A novel written in the first person works too: try *The Great Gatsby*.

Whatever you choose as the source material, ask your students to stage the scene (if you're using a play), or dramatise the extract (if you're using a book). If it's a book, all of the text should be retained, including and especially 'he said', 'she exclaimed', which should be spoken by the actor playing the character who goes on to speak or to exclaim whatever the line is.

However the group choose to stage the scene, they should establish a convention for moving from direct address to dialogue. This could be as simple as facing the audience in a presentational style for the direct address and facing the other actor(s) when delivering dialogue. Whatever the convention, it should be consistent throughout.

Exercise 42: Rearranging Chairs

An exercise to explore dynamic and stylised scene changes.

Ask the group to arrange four chairs in a row from upstage to downstage. For the purposes of this exercise, it does not matter whether all the chairs face downstage, face stage left, face stage right or a combination of directions. Regardless, the task is to experiment with different ways to rearrange the chairs into a row from stage left to stage right. They should play with having all four chairs occupied, then three, then two at the point the chair moving begins. They should also experiment with unison and cannon movement, including standing and sitting. Precision is important because it's so satisfying to watch. So, if something is supposedly being done in unison, rehearse it until it actually is done in unison. An appropriate piece of music will add atmosphere as well as a beat and a rhythm to work to.

The exercise is mechanistic – their only task is to establish a convention for rearranging the chairs. Why they are moving the chairs is not the point. The next stage is for the group to apply what they have discovered to how they make the transition from one scene to another, if that transition also requires transformation of the set. (I say 'set'. I really mean the limited number of chairs or rehearsal blocks you have allowed them. See Question 12 in Part 1: Preparation.)

Exercise 43: Image Building

A way of moving from scene to scene where no furniture moving is required, as well as exploring ways of entering and exiting. It's particularly useful for more abstract movement sequences but it is also for scenes that have several characters on stage at the start of the scene.

Ask the group to create an opening frozen image for the scene. (This may, of course, be a criterion you have given them for their piece or a convention they have decided on, anyway.) Now experiment with building it and deconstructing it, one person at a time.

It's also worth using this playing with animating and freezing as a way of starting and finishing scenes, and for the transitions between them. So, for example, ask the group to see what happens if a movement speeds up, slows down, or if an actor who is in the next scene freezes and is left on stage, transforming in plain sight?

By the way, leaving the stage should not mean vanishing from sight of the examiner. What is your convention – your house style – for being 'offstage'? Nine times out of ten, it should be in plain sight, frozen at the side watching the action or facing upstage at the back or side. Anything else looks sloppy and is unnecessary.

Everything is happening so fast it's incomprehensible! What can I do?

There is narrative economy and there is an underdeveloped idea. The two should not be confused. I have seen devised work where, in the first two minutes, the audience is bombarded with, say, a movement piece, statistics about something gory delivered in a Brechtian manner and three overwrought monologues. The purpose of each, other than for students to demonstrate that they knew certain techniques and were throwing them in, was unclear. The lack of development of each rendered them fairly incomprehensible. As the relevant student guidance sheet points out, an audience needs sufficient time to process and absorb what's going on.

It is worth asking students to experiment to determine:

- How slowly can they make a move?
- How long can they hold a pause?

The answers are, respectively, 'Very slowly so long as there is a sense of purpose which builds and holds the tension,' and 'A long time, so long as the pause is inhabited.'

So, if everything happens too fast and no moment is marked, that suggests the students are not fully connecting form and content and/or they do not know what the key moments in the narrative are. If it's the latter, see the suggestions in response to the final question, 'Is the narrative clear?'

However, the problem is often that students are simply delivering their lines too fast. People tend to speak faster when nervous. There are various simple and effective strategies for this, all of which can be applied in the final stage of the devising process, when the dialogue in the scene to be more or less finalised.

Exercise 44: Slowing Down

1. Run the scene, overarticulating every line. This helps with clarity but, usefully in this context, it obliges the student to speak more slowly too.

2. Ask the student to count 'one, two' aloud every time they reach a comma or semicolon in a speech. When they reach the end of a sentence, they should count 'one, two, three' aloud, whether the sentence concludes with a full stop, an exclamation mark or a question mark. (They may need to write the dialogue down, if they have not done so already, as part of their recording process.)

Next, run the same scene but this time the count is silent. Repeat as necessary until the student has internalised the need to pause, briefly, where the punctuation indicates it.

Does the work lack presence and a sense of occasion?

Listlessness, in rehearsal, in the showing of work in progress or – heaven forbid – in the final performance may be an indication of a lack of confidence and certainty about what they are doing and why. Throughout this part of the book there are exercises that address these points.

The sense of purpose that the next two exercises develop should boost confidence too but will also enhance your candidates' individual and collective stage presence. While it is true that some performers are more compelling than others, it is a mistake to assume that stage presence is one of those magical, 'got it or you ain't' qualities. (Patsy Rodenburg has written an entire book, *Presence*, on the subject.) Being present – that is to say, focused, committed and with an appropriate level of performance energy – is the basis of high attainment. These exercises support that, because they will train your students to regard stepping onto the stage as the start of a special event.

Both are best as teacher-led, whole-class activities, perhaps as the groups reach Stage 3 of the devising process.

Exercise 45: Crossing the Line

Ask the students to stand on one side of an imaginary line. As they step over the line, they should imagine that every part of their body is radiating presence or light or energy or confidence – what works best for the individual will vary. They should stand still once they have crossed the line. The point is not to demonstrate anything but to feel or visualise that inner presence. In their own time, students should experiment with moving backwards and forwards across that line, switching the performance energy on or off as they move backwards and forward.

The exercise is a simplified version of the 'psychological gesture' exercise developed by Michael Chekhov (nephew of the playwright).

Exercise 46: Taking the Applause

The whole group imagines they are the audience in the stalls of an enormous auditorium. Their favourite performer is about to appear to take her or his applause. The audience's task is to give that performer their unconditional adoration. As this should be expressed via applause, stamping, cheering, the activity can get very, very noisy – time its use appropriately if you don't want to upset colleagues in adjacent rooms!

One by one the entire group takes it in turns to be the favourite performer. There is an imaginary line between the wings and the stage. As they cross that line, they must feel suffused with confidence and energy. The audience *will* adore them. All they have to do is come centre stage, stand still, bow, acknowledge the applause and make eye contact with the audience, as well as with the audience beyond in the stalls, and in the dress circle, the gods and so on. Then exit.

This is surprisingly hard to do. Those who fidget, attempt to do too much because they do not feel that they are sufficiently interesting if standing still, avoid eye contact with the actual people present, should be made to do it again. In this way, the exercise also helps address the issue of doing too much.

Is the narrative clear?

This needs to be monitored throughout the refining stage of the process, as student resource sheet 4 and the structures themselves make clear. However, it's easy to lose your overview in amongst the detail, as tension mounts and the performance looms. To restore that overview, try the following:

Exercise 47: The Italian Version

(No, I don't know why it's called that!)

This exercise is extremely useful in the final stages of the rehearsal process in that it focuses the group's attention on the following questions:

- What's the main action in the scene?
- Why do I come on?
- Why do I leave?

The premise is that the narrative is reported rather than acted out. The performance group forms a circle. Even if your normal practice is for them to sit on the floor, allow chairs for this exercise: it makes the leaping up and down required easier. Each character comes on in the order of appearance in the piece. 'Comes on', for the purposes of this exercise, means that they stand and enters the circle and summarises what they do, in the present tense: 'I come on and I do – ' The sentence should summarise the action rather than what the character thinks or feels. Those in the scene remain standing in the circle, then exit in the appropriate order. Before each returns to their seat, they should state, 'I leave because – ' Continue, scene by scene, for the entire piece. Because no other dialogue or interaction is required, this will be an accelerated version.

Exercise 48: Marking the Key Moments

If any stage of the devising process has involved picking five key images with which to tell the story, this is a good point to revisit that exercise. Are the five key images still the same or are they different now that the piece is further down the line? Regardless, they are likely to be the key moments in the narrative. In which case, the piece can be reviewed and tweaked, if necessary, to ensure that those key moments are marked and that the build-up to each of these key moments is clear.

Preparation and Stimulus Material

Printable A4 versions of all these sheets can be downloaded
from www.nickhernbooks.co.uk/Making-Theatre

High-quality devised theatre is underpinned by effective group work. List five of the skills or personality types that you think are needed to create an effective rehearsal group.

1. _____

2. _____

3. _____

4. _____

5. _____

Bearing in mind your own strengths and weaknesses, state one person with whom you think you can work productively and one person with whom you think you cannot work productively. Your comments should focus on:

- Their skills and qualities rather than their personality.
- How working/not working with the people you name would improve your work and increase your skills in drama.

I would benefit from working with _____
because _____
_____

I would not benefit from working with _____
because _____
_____

Bearing in mind your own strengths and weaknesses, state one person that would benefit from working with you and one person that would not benefit from you.

_____ would benefit from working with me
because _____
_____

_____ would not benefit from working with me
because _____
_____

When reviewing your schemes of work, ask yourself the following questions:

- Are there opportunities for increasingly long and independent rehearsal processes in preparation for the devised theatre requirements of your exam specification?

- Are there opportunities to develop an understanding that process has worth in and of itself, and that rehearsal involves experimentation and discovery, not just getting it right first time and moving on?

- Are there exercises and activities that enable students to develop understanding of different approaches to characterisation, including how such concepts as status inform characterisation?

- Are there exercises and activities that analyse dramatic structure, in particular what makes an effective beginning for a piece and how to sustain the audience's attention?

- Are there exercises and activities that will enable students to understand that revealing through action is more dramatically effective than telling through speech?

- What opportunities do students have to see theatre (whether trips to the theatre, visiting theatre companies or GCSE/A-level/BTEC work by older or other students)?

- What opportunities do students have to perform, whether to other classes or to other audiences?

- What opportunities do students have to understand the conventions of various theatrical genres and apply these to their own practical work?

- Generally, teachers stress the responsibilities of the audience: to be attentive and supportive. At what point do students become aware that the performer has responsibilities too? (Such as audibility, configuration of space, performance energy and commitment.)

- What opportunities are there for students to recognise and demonstrate their understanding of the medium and elements of Drama within their work and how these can assist and clarify dramatic form?

ENSURING BOYS' ATTAINMENT

Boys respond well to physical tasks.	
Boys prefer comedy, perhaps as a defence mechanism to avoid working in depth or revealing emotion.	
Boys are resistant to starting tasks.	
Boys' responses are raw or literal, whereas girls' responses are more considered.	
Girls discuss and plan for longer; boys stand up sooner.	
Boys take longer to settle.	
Boys get over conflict more quickly than girls. Boys don't hold grudges or, if they do, they mask the fact, as an acceptable social response.	
Boys' written work (and verbal evaluation) is weaker than girls'.	
Boys are more confident with physical work and more able to take risks.	
Boys like competition. They want to win, but don't want to lose face so may not participate through fear of failure.	
Boys love and need praise.	
Boys prefer an immediate response. They are not so good at deferred gratification – hence a sustained rehearsal period is inherently problematic.	
Boys are more delicate than girls with regard to criticism.	
Boys are worse at listening to instructions. (A statistic claims boys can't hold more than three instructions at one time.)	
Boys are not as good at abstract work.	
Boys cannot concentrate for as long as girls.	
Boys are better at performing aggressive emotions and at stage fighting.	
Boys are less enthusiastic readers: words equal work.	

They stood by the window
And watched the old church
Burn for the second time.
The light from the fire
Made her glow like an angel
As she pulled him down and smiled.
They lay on the bed,
There were shouts all around
They could shut the whole war out.
With the squeak of the springs
And tomorrow's dreams
And the beating of their hearts.

He would lay his arms down for her.
She would forgive his brother's crime.
They would do anything
To make it past Vrbana Bridge.

Well he looked up to Jesus
And she looked to the east
Where the sun was soon to rise.
She asked for Allah's blessings
To keep them both alive.
They had friends in high places
Who could do them a favour,
Turn a blind eye.
They'd seen so much hate
And death every day,
'Let's just let those two walk by'.

They would lay their arms down for her.
They would forgive his brother's crime.
Just for one moment they would
Let them pass Vrbana Bridge.

Through a crack in the wall
Of a sandbagged building
The soldier saw them fall.
He said, 'If love was their only armour
It did no good at all.'
They lay for six days
In a final embrace.
They had shut the whole war out.
The soldier blames the other side
But even he has his doubts.

He would lay down his arms down for her
He would forgive his brother's crime
He would lay down his arms
To let them pass Vrbana Bridge.

Someone must have been telling lies about Josef K., he knew he had done nothing wrong but, one morning, he was arrested. Every day at eight in the morning he was brought his breakfast by Mrs Grubach's cook – Mrs Grubach was his landlady – but today she didn't come. That had never happened before.

K. waited a little while, looked from his pillow at the old woman who lived opposite and who was watching him with an inquisitiveness quite unusual for her, and finally, both hungry and disconcerted, rang the bell. There was immediately a knock at the door and a man entered. He had never seen the man in this house before. He was slim but firmly built, his clothes were black and close-fitting, with many folds and pockets, buckles and buttons and a belt, all of which gave the impression of being very practical but without making it very clear what they were actually for.

'Who are you?' asked K., sitting half upright in his bed. The man, however, ignored the question as if his arrival simply had to be accepted, and merely replied, 'You rang?' 'Anna should have brought me my breakfast,' said K. He tried to work out who the man actually was, first in silence, just through observation and by thinking about it, but the man didn't stay still to be looked at for very long. Instead he went over to the door, opened it slightly, and said to someone who was clearly standing immediately behind it, 'He wants Anna to bring him his breakfast.'

There was a little laughter in the neighbouring room, it was not clear from the sound of it whether there were several people laughing. The strange man could not have learned anything from it that he hadn't known already, but now he said to K., as if making his report 'It is not possible.'

'It would be the first time that's happened,' said K., as he jumped out of bed and quickly pulled on his trousers. 'I want to see who that is in the next room, and why it is that Mrs Grubach has let me be disturbed in this way.' It immediately occurred to him that he needn't have said this out loud, and that he must to some extent have acknowledged their authority by doing so, but that didn't seem important to him at the time. That, at least, is how the stranger took it, as he said, 'Don't you think you'd better stay where you are?'

'I want neither to stay here nor to be spoken to by you until you've introduced yourself.'

'I meant it for your own good,' said the stranger and opened the door, this time without being asked.

We All Come From Somewhere Else
INTERVIEW QUESTIONS

- When did you come to [*wherever you live now*] and why?

- What were your first impressions when you arrived?

- How did your parents meet?

- What's the most frightening experience you've ever had?

- What was the happiest day of your life, so far?

- What was the saddest day of your life, so far?

- What were your school days like?

- Were your parents strict?

- What is the biggest change you have seen since your childhood?

- Who lived in your house before you?

- How did you meet your partner?

Additional questions:

1.

2.

3.

I expected something beautiful but at the time it was very very dirty and everything seemed to be so black. We were very distressed. We arrived about half-past eleven in the evening. It was raining – awful, terrible weather it was.

I was very homesick. It looked very different. It was a big city and I come from a very small island. I was a bit confused. The first time I went on the Underground I got lost.

My friend came to meet me at Waterloo. The scene was just a lot of people. Everybody who come off the train and who come to meet relatives. So it was just a big crowd of people.

There was curious onlookers standing around looking: anxious black people and curious white people.

I was on the train and when I looked out through the window and see all these little houses and outside is so black, I said to somebody, 'When are we going to reach England?'

My husband came to meet me, everything was strange.

Nowhere to live, nowhere to sleep, nowhere – nobody wanted to know you. If I had money I would have gone back straight away.

When you arrive, people try to communicate with you through sign language or they shout at you. They think perhaps by shouting they can make you understand what they are talking about.

It was a feeling of total confusion having to go through immigration and all the people around you that you didn't know. I felt utterly despairing. It was a feeling of total confusion because I suddenly realised I'd arrived, I'd left home and I arrived here.

I cried like a baby the first week I was here. You had to be at work by 6.30 a.m. If you were late you would be disciplined.

At the time you used to get signs saying, 'No Irish, no Blacks'. You know, that saddened me, coming from a place where they tell you this is the mother country.

You had to keep your dignity. A lot of boys came here and had mental breakdowns because of that stress.

PAIR EXERCISE (A) AND TRIO EXERCISE

Pair Exercise (A)

A is a person packing up a room (this is mimed, of course). No dialogue. B is another character who is watching. The pair need to experiment to decide:

- Whether B is present from the start.
- Whether B is standing or sitting.
- Whether A acknowledges B's presence in any way during the scene.

When A is finished, they pause for five seconds precisely. B says to A: 'It's time to go now.'

A does not respond.

Trio Exercise

Prepare the following sequence of movements. No dialogue should be added.

- There are three chairs.
- A is walking up and down.
- B enters and sits on one chair. They tap their foot, repeatedly.
- C enters. A keeps walking up and down, B keeps tapping.
- C exits.
- D enters.
- B stands.
- D takes B's seat.
- A pauses. Then continues walking up and down.
- B exits.
- C enters again. Sits on another chair.
- D and C make eye contact.
- A stops walking. Opens their mouth, as if about to speak. The scene ends at this point.

Solo Exercise (A)

There is an empty chair in an empty room. A person walks in and sits on the chair. The rest of the group watch, then suggest:

- Who is the person? For instance: old, young, high or low status?
- Where is the person? Is it a familiar place or a strange place?
- What has just happened?
- What is about to happen?
- What is the person feeling? How can we tell?

Pair Exercise (B)

A. Well?

B *does not respond.*

A. Well?

B *does not respond.*

A. Did you go there?

There is a pause. B *nods.*

B. I found this note. (*Reads the following.*) 'I am what I am. I see the nature of my offence. It is finished. It is finished.'

Pair Exercise (C)

The pair sits opposite each other. They have a muttered conversation. They can talk gibberish, if they wish: the point is that the audience do not know what they are saying and, at this point, the actors do not need to know what or who is being discussed.

Stipulate that there will be three pauses. The pair should work out when. During each pause, each person should look left or look right or look up or look down. They could both do the same but do not have to. The looks might be simultaneous but do not have to be. One might be in response to the other. The pair should not make any decisions about why the pause or why the look in whatever direction: the point, as with preceding activities, is to allow the audience to interpret what is going on and, perhaps, why.

The character mimes the following in the specified order. They may refer to the list of instructions as they do so: the purpose is not to test their memory but to see what the sequence suggests, both to the performer and to those watching. For this reason, it is useful to have someone who can read the sequence out so that, the first time through, the performer does not know what comes next.

The character:

- Sits (and remains so until the ninth action in the sequence).
- Smokes.
- Glance over to a bed.
- Coughs.
- Lifts handkerchief to mouth.
- Looks at handkerchief.
- Throws cigarette on table.
- Coughs.
- Stands.
- Goes to bed (to look at whoever is there, not to sleep).
- Bends.
- Kisses whoever is in bed.
- Goes to mirror.

The sequence should be performed twice: neutrally the first time then, the second time through, with whatever mood or emotion seems appropriate to the performer.

The Third Way
'PIRATE JENNY'

You people can watch while I'm
  scrubbing these floors
And I'm scrubbin the floors while
  you're gawking.
Maybe once ya tip me and it makes ya
  feel swell
In this crummy southern town
In this crummy old hotel
But you'll never guess to who you're
  talkin.
No. You couldn't ever guess to who
  you're talkin.
Then one night there's a scream in
  the night
And you'll wonder who could that
  have been?
And you see me kinda grinnin while
  I'm scrubbin
And you say, what's she got to grin?
I'll tell you.
There's a ship,
The black freighter
With a skull on its masthead
Will be coming in.
You gentlemen can say, 'Hey gal,
  finish them floors!
Get upstairs! What's wrong with you!
  Earn your keep here!'
You toss me your tips
And look out to the ships
But I'm counting your heads
As I'm making the beds
Cuz there's nobody gonna sleep here,
  honey.
Nobody – Nobody!
Then one night there's a scream in
  the night
And you say, 'Who's that kicking up a
  row?'
And ya see me kinda starin out the
  winda
And you say, 'What's she got to stare
  at now?'
I'll tell ya.
There's a ship,
The black freighter
Turns around in the harbour
Shootin guns from her bow.
Now you gentlemen can wipe off that
  smile off your face

Cause every building in town is a flat
  one.
This whole frickin place will be down
  to the ground.
Only this cheap hotel standing up
  safe and sound
And you yell, 'Why do they spare that
  one?'
Yes.
That's what you say.
'Why do they spare that one?'
All the night through, through the
  noise and to-do
You wonder who is that person that
  lives up there?
And you see me stepping out in the
  morning
Looking nice with a ribbon in my hair.
And the ship,
The black freighter
Runs a flag up its masthead
And a cheer rings the air.
By noontime the dock
Is a-swarmin with men
Comin out from the ghostly freighter.
They move in the shadows
Where no one can see
And they're chainin up people
And they're bringin em to me
Askin me,
'Kill them now, or later?'
Askin me!
'Kill them now, or later?'
Noon by the clock
And so still by the dock
You can hear a foghorn miles away.
And in that quiet of death
I'll say, 'Right now.
Right now!'
Then they'll pile up the bodies
And I'll say,
'That'll learn ya!'
And the ship,
The black freighter
Disappears out to sea
And
On – It – Is – Me

Same Starting Point, Different Outcomes
NOTICE OF CHANGE OF NAME

From the *Stratford Gazette*, 20th March 1915

I formally, wholly, absolutely and utterly renounce, relinquish and abandon the Christian and Surname of Carl Schneider.

I declare that I have assumed, adopted and determined and I intend henceforth, upon all occasions whatsoever to use and subscribe myself by the name of Charles Bennett instead of Carl Schneider.

Dated this 17th day of March 1915

Charles Bennett (Formerly known as Carl Schneider)

MILITARY DRILL

- Attention.
- Present arms.
- Shoulder arms.
- Stand at ease.
- Right turn (or left turn).
- Quick march.
- At ease.
- Fall out.

No Feeling, No Emotion
VARNADO SIMPSON'S ACCOUNT

That day in My Lai, I was personally responsible for killing about twenty-five people. Personally. Men, women. From shooting them, to cutting their throats, scalping them, to . . . cutting off their hands and cutting out their tongues. I did it.

I just went. My mind just went. And I wasn't the only one that did it. A lot of other people did it. I just killed. Once I started, the – the training, the whole programming part of killing, it just came out.

A lot of people were doing it. I just followed suit. I just lost all sense of direction, of purpose. I just started killing any kinda way I could kill. It just came. I didn't know I had it in me.

After I killed the child, my whole mind just went. It just went. And once you start, it's very easy to keep on. Once you start. The hardest – the part that's hard is to kill, but once you kill, that becomes easier, to kill the next person and the next one and the next one. Because I had no feelings and no emotions or no nothing. No direction. I just killed.

No Feeling, No Emotion
MY LAI: TESTIMONY

'I gave them a good boy and they made him a murderer.'
GI's mother

'We had orders, but the orders we had was that we were going into an enemy village and that they was well armed. I didn't find that when I got there. And ordering me to shoot down innocent people, that's not an order – that's craziness to me, you know. And so I don't feel like I have to obey that.'
Harry Stanley, Charlie Company

'We were kids, eighteen, nineteen years old. I was twenty-one years old at the time. I was one of the oldest people around there among the common grunts.
Most of them [Charlie Company] had never been away from home before they went into the service. And they end up in Vietnam, many of them because they thought they were going to do something courageous on behalf of their country. Here are these guys who have gone in and in a moment, in a moment, following orders, in a context in which they'd been trained, prepared to follow orders, they do what they're told, and they shouldn't have, and they look back a day later and realise they probably made the biggest mistake of their lives. [There were] only a few extraordinary people who were in those circumstances who had the presence of mind and strength of their own character that would see them through. Most people didn't. And for most of them – people that I was personally just stunned to discover had made the wrong choice they did – they all had to live with it. They had to live with it. And so do we all.'
Ronald Ridenhour, GI not with Charlie Company

'When my troops were getting massacred and mauled by an enemy I couldn't see, I couldn't feel and I couldn't touch, nobody in the military system ever described them as anything other than Communism. They didn't give it a race, they didn't give it a sex, they didn't give it an age. They never let me believe it was just a philosophy in a man's mind that was my enemy out there.'
Lt William Calley's final speech to his court martial

'I think of it all the time, and that is why I am old before my time. I remember it all the time. I think about it and I can't sleep. I'm all alone and life is hard and there's no one I can turn to for help. Then I think of it all the time. I'm always sad and unhappy, and that's why I'm old.
I think of my daughter and my mother, both of them dead. I won't forgive. I hate them very much. I won't forgive them as long as I live. Think of those children, that small . . . Those children still at their mothers' breasts being killed . . . I hate them very much . . .
I miss my mother, my sister, my children. I think of them lying dead. I think of it and feel my insides being cut to pieces.'
Truong Thi Lee, who lost nine members of her family in the massacre

Rehearsing is not about getting it right. That's the exact opposite of what it's for. I always say straight off, get up and try something. It's better. Because you may find something quite interesting that emerges in that stage. You often get people saying no to someone's idea before they've tried it. You say, 'Have you tried this?' 'No, no, that won't work.' Well, you don't know until you've tried it. It may be a brilliant idea. It might not be. But I always think you should try every idea. You've got to try it. And you can only know by doing it. You can't know by talking about it.

Paul Hunter, Told by an Idiot

Index of Exercises

1.   Breathing   158

2.   Articulation   159

3.   Vocal Clarity   161

4.   Volume   162

5.   Physical Approaches to Characterisation   164

6.   Vocabularies   166

7.   'How (Not) To . . .'   167

8.   What's My Objective?   168

9.   What's My Intention?   168

10.   'Before the Scene Started, I . . .'   170

11.   A Personal Source   171

12.   Storytelling   172

13.   Transformation   173

14.   Triggering   174

15.   Appropriated Gesture   175

16.   Magnifying the Gesture   175

17.   The Beaufort Scale   176

18.   Pass the Emotion   176

19.   Sticky Feet   177

20.   Convalescence   177

21.   House on a Mountain Top   178

22.   Don't Enter the Triangle!   179

23.   Playing the Cross   179

24.   Energy Clap   182

25.   Cherry Picking   183

26.   Attuning   184

27.   The Imagined Listener   185

28.   Distraction Through Action   187

29.   Understanding Subtext   189

30.   Playing the Routine   190

31.   The Yes/No Game   191

32.   Game, Set and Match   191

33. Tug of War   192

34. Web of Intimacy   192

35. Distillation and Paring Down   193

36. The Emperor Game   194

37. 'Is There Anybody There?' 195

38. Anticipation   195

39. Fun Run   196

40. How to Bank Emotion 197

41. From First Person to Third Person   198

42. Rearranging Chairs   199

43. Image Building   200

44. Slowing Down   201

45. Crossing the Line   202

46. Taking the Applause 203

47. The Italian Version   203

48. Marking the Key Moments 204

www.nickhernbooks.co.uk

facebook.com/nickhernbooks

twitter.com/nickhernbooks